Video in Teacher Learning

*To my mom, Rhoda Kramer, who always wanted a book dedicated to her—
no one was a keener or more honest observer of herself and human nature.*

*And to my amazing family—how did I get so lucky? Ted, Zachary, Jacob and Rianna.
Thanks for your patience while mom was on her laptop.*

Video in Teacher Learning

Through Their Own Eyes

Laura Baecher

A JOINT PUBLICATION

FOR INFORMATION:

Corwin

A SAGE Company

2455 Teller Road

Thousand Oaks, California 91320

(800) 233-9936

www.corwin.com

SAGE Publications Ltd.

1 Oliver's Yard

55 City Road

London EC1Y 1SP

United Kingdom

SAGE Publications India Pvt. Ltd.

B 1/I 1 Mohan Cooperative Industrial Area

Mathura Road, New Delhi 110 044

India

SAGE Publications Asia-Pacific Pte. Ltd.

18 Cross Street #10-10/11/12

China Square Central

Singapore 048423

Program Director and Publisher: Dan Alpert

Content Development Editor: Lucas Schleicher

Senior Editorial Assistant: Mia Rodriguez

Production Editor: Andrew Olson

Copy Editor: Karin Rathert

Typesetter: C&M Digitals (P) Ltd.

Proofreader: Eleni-Maria Georgiou

Indexer: Robie Grant

Cover Designer: Candice Harman

Marketing Manager: Sharon Pendergast

Library of Congress Cataloging-in-Publication Data

Names: Baecher, Laura Hope, author.

Title: Video in teacher learning : through their own eyes / Laura Baecher.

Description: Thousand Oaks, California : Corwin/ICLE, 2019. | Includes bibliographical references and index.

Identifiers: LCCN 2019004945 | ISBN 9781544337258 (pbk. : alk. paper)

Subjects: LCSH: Teachers—In-service training—Audio-visual aids. | Teachers—Training of—Audio-visual aids. | Teacher effectiveness—Evaluation. | Video tapes in education.

Classification: LCC LB1731 .B234 2019 | DDC 370.71/1—dc23

LC record available at https://lccn.loc.gov/2019004945

This book is printed on acid-free paper.

Certified Chain of Custody
Promoting Sustainable Forestry
www.sfiprogram.org
SFI-01268

SFI label applies to text stock

19 20 21 22 23 10 9 8 7 6 5 4 3 2 1

CONTENTS

Chapter 1 • Why Video for Teacher Learning?   3

This chapter highlights the research base that strongly supports
video as a tool in developing teachers' observation skills, presents
video in teacher learning along a continuum of development,
offers considerations in the design of video analysis tasks, and
describes the types of facilitation structures often used with video
for teacher learning.

Chapter 2 • What Observation Skills Need to Be in Place Before I Get Started With Video?   15

This chapter connects the ways we think to how we observe
classrooms, shares considerations for promoting nonjudgmental,
evidence-based observation, and outlines a set of observation
skills that will be useful in video analysis of teaching.

Chapter 3 • How Does the Way We Communicate Support Learning With Video?   35

This chapter highlights why video can make teachers feel
particularly vulnerable in the learning process, presents
considerations for listening and speaking when engaging
in conversations based on video observation, and identifies
strategies and communicative moves that maximize the learning
for teachers from the video review process.

Chapter 4 • What Are the Technical Aspects of Creating Video Recordings of Teaching?   47

This chapter reviews best practices in capturing, editing, storing,
and sharing video of teaching and provides sample consent and
permission forms that respect and protect teachers and students.

Visit the companion website at
http://resources.corwin.com/ VideoinTeacherLearning
for downloadable resources.

ACKNOWLEDGMENTS

With appreciation both professional and personal, this book builds on the foundation of my mentors in the art and science of humanistic teacher observation—John Fanselow and Bob Oprandy. I would never have taken this path without you lighting the way.

Special gratitude to Hunter College for supporting video analysis of teaching early on and continually reinvesting in teacher learning that is relevant and thoughtful. I am ever in your debt: Jennifer Raab, David Steiner, Sherryl Browne Graves, David Connor, Jenny Tuten, Yang Hu, Michael Middleton, and Matthew Caballero.

To all the educators who have worked with me and bravely examined themselves, teaching and learning through video reflection—you teach me more than I could ever teach you.

And to copyeditor Karin Rathert and the caring, insightful, and supportive editorial staff at Corwin—Dan Alpert, Mia Rodriguez, and Lucas Schleicher—thank you for giving me wings for my first solo flight.

PUBLISHER'S ACKNOWLEDGMENTS

Corwin gratefully acknowledges the contributions of the following reviewers:

Kami Christensen
Instructional Coach Trainer, Curriculum Specialist
Nebo School District
Spanish Fork, UT

Trish Gooch
Instructional Coach
TG Coaching
Wangaratta, VIC, Australia

Eric C. Lee
Director
Jacksonville State University Inservice Center
Anniston, AL

Isabel Sawyer
Regional Director
Center for the Collaborative Classroom
Alameda, CA

Elaine Shobert
Curriculum Coordinator
Rock Rest Elementary School
Monroe, NC

Nicolette Smith
K–12 Professional Learning Facilitator
Northwest Regional Professional Development Program
Reno, NV

Marisa Ramirez Stukey
Regional Director
Center for the Collaborative Classroom
Alameda, CA

Kim Tucker
Supervisor of Curriculum, Principal
Somers Point School District
Somers Point, NJ

David Vernot
Curriculum Consultant
Butler County Educational Service Center
Hamilton, OH

REFERENCE LIST: 20 VIDEO ANALYSES OF TEACHING TASKS

Chapter	VAT Task	Focus	Level
5	**Selective verbatim** → Involves verbatim scripting in tandem with a chosen focus, in this case, teacher question types.	Questioning	Introductory
	Interactional flow → Engages viewers in talk-mapping to explore interaction patterns in the lesson.	Source and target of classroom talk	Introductory
	Time sampling → Uses time intervals to collect data around students' behavior working in a group.	Student interaction in peer learning	Introductory
	Tallying → Examines various uses of teacher praise.	Use of praise	Introductory
6	**Virtual grand rounds** → Video clips are used to spark a focused investigation of a particular practice across several classrooms.	Giving instructions	Introductory
	Conversation analysis → Segments of video related to classroom talk are transcribed and examined for deeper student and teacher roles.	Classroom discussion	Intermediate
	Student perspective video → The camera is placed close to a student/students so their point of view is captured.	Student thinking	Intermediate
	Student work with video analysis → Teachers combine review of student work with video records from the lesson.	Teacher modeling	Intermediate

(Continued)

(Continued)

Chapter	VAT Task	Focus	Level
7	*Lesson de-/reconstruction* → Teachers watch a video of a lesson and try to construct the lesson plan that went with it.	Lesson design	Introductory
	Video-infused lesson study → Teacher pairs or triads carry out lesson study and then video their delivered lessons, returning to debrief while sharing videos.	Use of technology	Intermediate
	Video-based learning walks → Both video clips and student work from the same lesson are reviewed together for deeper insights into student learning.	Academic language	Advanced
	Collaborative inquiry for leaders of teacher learning → School leaders or teacher educators share their viewpoints from different disciplinary angles.	Sharing expertise	Advanced
8	*Think-aloud playback* → Coaches/ supervisors invite teachers to engage in a think-aloud protocol while they watch a replay of a lesson, as a form of dynamic assessment.	Differentiated instruction	Advanced
	Video-enhanced instructional coaching → Coaches/supervisors use video to support collaborative coaching conversations about a teacher's growth.	Response opportunities	Advanced
	Live-streaming video coaching → Streaming video is relayed live to a coach who provides on-the-spot suggestions through bug-in-ear technology.	Classroom management	Advanced
	Supervisor/Coach collaborative development → Those who carry out mentoring or feedback conversations with teachers video record those conversations and examine their talk with a peer or supervising mentor.	Feedback conversations	Advanced

Chapter	VAT Task	Focus	Level
9	**Calibration of observers** → The use of video to support inter-rater reliability among a number of observers.	Knowledge of students	Advanced
	Self-assessment via video → Teachers are trained on the use of a viewing rubric and then apply that rubric to evaluate their own practice	Student higher-order discussion	Advanced
	Distance supervision → Teachers submit video to coaches/supervisors who are situated remotely and receive evaluative feedback.	Student engagement in mathematics	Advanced
	Video in teacher portfolios → Teachers submit video and video analysis to supervisors who then score the lesson and the reflection as part of a formal teacher evaluation system.	Lesson evaluation	Advanced

ABOUT THE AUTHOR

Dr. Laura Baecher is faculty in the School of Education at Hunter College, City University of New York. She has been a teacher and teacher educator for over 25 years, and her research relates to teacher preparation, teacher leadership, supervision, and the use of video for teacher learning. She works closely with New York City public schools and has consulted with a variety of districts and colleges of teacher education in the use of video for teacher coaching.

LAYING THE GROUNDWORK FOR POWERFUL USE OF VIDEO IN TEACHER LEARNING

No matter our educational role—whether teacher, teacher leader, coach, administrator, researcher, or teacher educator—video can be leveraged as an important tool in understanding and improving classroom practice. No other observation instrument offers the chance for us to see ourselves in action, or freeze the fast-paced moments of classroom interactions. However, there are several elements that are essential to appreciate before entering into using video to facilitate teacher learning—one's own or the learning of others.

In the first part of this text, foundational skills in non-judgmental classroom observation, awareness of bias, and thoughtful interpersonal interaction are among the aspects to consider in order to successfully lead teacher professional learning using video analysis of teaching. In Part 2, specific video analysis tasks are presented in detail, to be selectively adopted and adapted for use in your context.

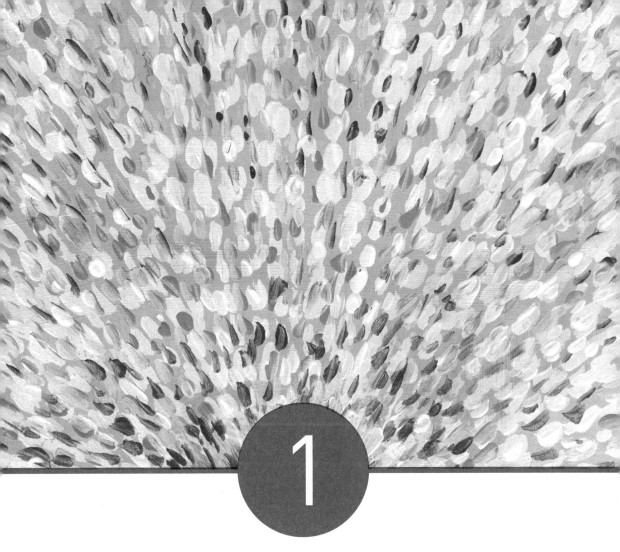

1

WHY VIDEO FOR
TEACHER LEARNING?

When I discover who I am, I'll be free.

—Ralph Ellison, *Invisible Man*

CHAPTER OBJECTIVES

- To highlight the research base that strongly supports video as a tool in developing teachers' observation skills
- To present video in teacher learning along a continuum of development
- To offer considerations in the design of video analysis tasks
- To describe the types of facilitation structures often used with video for teacher learning

Take a moment and try to imagine these scenarios:

1. An artist completes her painting and shares it with her instructor in order to improve her craft. The painting is then taken away where neither the artist nor her instructor can see it again. When they speak about the painting, the instructor and artist rely solely on their memory and do not look at the painting while they speak. The written feedback the artist later receives on the painting is in the form of a rubric with 35 categories in which the instructor has rated her, without seeing the painting again, from 1 to 4.

2. A nurse learns about how to determine a patient's level of risk in an intake procedure he has to perform. He now must do this procedure himself with a patient in a clinic, and the nurse educator is going to be there to observe him in this fieldwork setting to give him feedback on how he carries it out. However, he has never seen anyone do the procedure; he has only read a description of it in a textbook and heard his instructor and others discuss it in class.

3. A teacher is told that she needs to improve her practice in the area of student engagement. Several administrators, mentor teachers, and coaches all observe the teacher and conduct numerous conferences with the teacher to explain to her what she needs to do better. She tries her best to understand what it is that she needs to change, but each observer notices different areas and gives different suggestions.

The first two scenarios above seem implausible, yet the third scenario may seem quite familiar and thus, believable. What all three share in common is the notion that complex professional skills can be acquired just by reading about them, having them described to us, or by receiving feedback based on our imperfect memory. What is missing in all three scenarios is the active and direct ownership of observing the skills or products in question by the very professionals who are carrying them out. Unfortunately, this is precisely what we do when we learn to teach—or support teachers in their learning—without ever looking directly at our own or others' teaching.

Teaching is incredibly complex, and no matter how much teachers try to attend to learners and learning while teaching and no matter how much feedback observers give them, analysis of teaching relies too often on fragmented recollections of events filtered through the viewer's perspective. Video is the ideal tool to turn that around. Analysis of teaching via video supports reflective, critical inquiry because of its stop, rewind, and re-view capacity, and it opens up possibilities for seeing other teachers and ourselves teaching. Video is the only means by which teachers can see their teaching through their own eyes.

Due to its tremendous potential for teacher learning, the analysis of teaching via video records has been in existence for many years, and the accessibility and portability of digital video has made it ever easier for teachers to utilize. However, greater facility and access have not always led to thoughtful, descriptive review of instruction, as the process of video analysis must be carefully scaffolded. Coaches, supervisors, mentors, teacher leaders, teacher educators, and facilitators of professional learning communities recognize how powerful sharing video clips of teaching can be yet quickly come to the realization that a foundation first needs to be laid for teachers to gain the most from the experience. Often, facilitators are unsure about how to create such structures and seek protocols that will guide them in leading teacher learning with video analysis. This book seeks to address these concerns by providing educators with concrete, user-friendly protocols that share descriptive viewing practices designed to support teachers and facilitators in effective video analysis.

This book begins by articulating research-based principles for selecting, introducing, and leading professional learning that incorporates video analysis. Understanding the research base for the use of video in teacher learning provides a solid foundation for entering into the process of designing and facilitating teacher-learning experiences with video.

WHAT IS THE RESEARCH BASE FOR THE USE OF VIDEO IN TEACHER LEARNING?

Video began to be discussed in the research literature on teacher learning in the early 1970s. Its use has increased as a result of improved accessibility of digital video recording, storing, and sharing, and there are now numerous studies published on its applications. Video analysis has especially been the focus of research since the early 1990s, and as a still-emerging technological tool in teacher learning, research on its applications is helpful for educators who want to optimize its application. Understanding promising practices in the use of video for teacher learning has become increasingly important in light of the general movement in the United States toward more practice-based, clinically rich teacher education (Grossman, 2010) and toward more evidence-based teacher professional learning in K–12 school districts.

This research base indicates that video analysis is an activity that takes place across the whole spectrum of teacher learning, from preservice to in-service teacher-learning contexts, across all disciplinary boundaries, and in the education of teachers in diverse content areas.

Consistent Findings From the Research Show That	
Video analysis of teaching is most meaningful when it is highly scaffolded.	In order for classroom observation to have shared meaning, observers must share a common vocabulary of looking at classrooms. This is a vital step in the analysis of teaching, whether on video or live, that is often overlooked. Especially for novice teachers (Yadav & Koehler, 2007), gradual introduction to a variety of concepts with video illustrations builds teachers' shared understanding.
Video analysis of teaching generates a sense of cognitive dissonance.	Video is uniquely suited to generating a sense of cognitive dissonance between teachers' beliefs and what they see occurring, which can lead to new ways of thinking. As Rosaen, Lundeberg, Cooper, Fritzen, and Terpstra (2008) state, "Dissonance does not need to be negative to lead to learning; it just needs to jar complacency" (p. 358).
Video analysis of teaching supports teachers' development of noticing and reflection skills.	Video materials provide a powerful source of evidence for the development of noticing skills (Marsh & Mitchell, 2014) and honest, deep reflection on teaching (Tripp & Rich, 2012) and can even promote critical consciousness and self-awareness (Schieble, Vetter, & Meacham, 2015).
Video analysis allows for the development of shared understandings of practice.	Video is an effective medium for grounding multiple perspectives within a process of reviewing data, leading to "configurational validity" (Goldman-Segall, 1995). Shared video review between observers and teachers directly impacts the nature of their post-observation conversations (Baecher & McCormack, 2015) and allows for dynamic assessment of teacher thinking. Video also creates opportunities for educators at a distance to share practice (Alexander, Williams, & Nelson, 2012).
Video analysis impacts teacher skill development.	Video analysis shows positive effects on skill development, which can be attributed to the combination of the video feedback along with observation viewers' guides that direct the educators' attention to particular micro-skills (Fukkink, Trienekens, & Kramer, 2011; Nagro & Cornelius, 2013).
Video analysis supports norm-referenced self-evaluation.	Teachers who have engaged in video analysis and then are asked to self-evaluate their practice provide more evidence and score themselves with greater fidelity to observation criteria than those who use memory-based recall (Baecher, Kung, Jewkes, & Rosalia, 2013), and video-based self-evaluation can suppress inflation or misperceptions of one's effectiveness in discrete categories of performance.

In spite of the abundance of research pointing to the benefits of video analysis in teacher learning, one persistent gap exists: specific, practical guidelines for those who want to engage in video for teacher learning. In Orland-Barak and Maskit's

(2017) recent review of research on video analysis in teacher learning, they note that "there are very few studies that focus on how mediating learning through and from video examination is actually implemented and applied in teaching" (p. 53). They call for an outlining of thoughtful facilitation processes within a "video-based pedagogy" (p. 56).

What are those thoughtful facilitation moves actually employed by those who lead video analysis with teachers? This is the purpose of this text—to offer better understanding of *how* video analysis can be conducted. Clarity in the details of video analysis activities depends on first identifying the stage of learning the teachers are at, the purpose of the video analysis, and then choosing from an array of approaches to guide the video review.

WHAT KINDS OF VIDEO ANALYSIS MAKE SENSE FOR TEACHERS AT DIFFERENT STAGES OF THEIR LEARNING?

Video analysis of teaching can be situated at various points, for different purposes, across the continuum of teacher learning. Although there are foundational aspects to becoming more skilled at observation, the process is not strictly linear, for as we attempt new approaches, we often have to return to pure description to ensure that we are "noticing" and using the data that video provides rather than our impressionistic memories. Each time the focus changes or the state of teacher learning changes, the type of video analysis that takes place is impacted.

Video can first be introduced to teachers in order to *learn how to look at teaching and learning*. This involves ways of carrying out classroom observations that address specific, observable elements of universal classroom practices learning in ways that are descriptive and non-evaluative. For instance, teachers might repeatedly view short clips to tally how many students are talking or how many questions the teacher poses. These types of "noticing tasks" preempt judgment and maximize the potential of video, which offers the possibility to rewind and replay in order to collect accurate data.

Teachers might then move on in video analysis to *learn how to look at specific practices*. Specific viewing targets might be methods, approaches, or routines that are particular to certain discipline areas. The viewing focus could also be a common professional teaching dilemma that can trigger discussion or cross-disciplinary concepts that are helpful to see in action: "culturally relevant pedagogy," or "student-centered learning." It is important to note that these stages ideally precede teachers' implementation of these methods or approaches. These first two stages can support the fieldwork and observation stages in preservice teacher learning and the need for baseline norming in-service educator learning experiences.

"Learning what my learners and I look like" utilizes video clips of teachers' own practices in a variety of ways and for a range of purposes. For instance, teachers may wish to simply explore pupil behavior in order to better understand how a particular learner or group activity is taking place or to investigate their own teacher talk. The descriptive, nonjudgmental orientation to video analysis should be established as firmly as possibly before entering into this phase so that the teacher will be able to discover as much as possible in the video rather than adopting a self-judgment lens. Ideally, teachers become skilled observers of classroom interactions

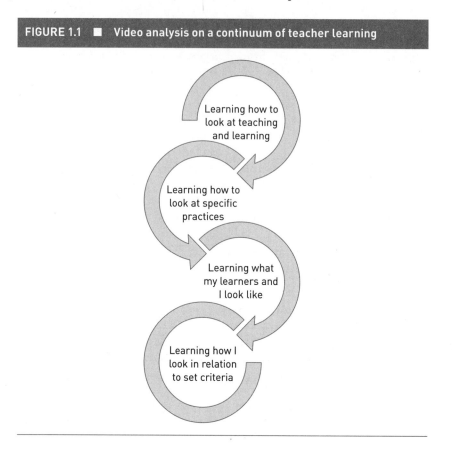

FIGURE 1.1 ■ Video analysis on a continuum of teacher learning

before they are asked to view a clip of their own practice and determine "strengths" and "areas for improvement."

At times, however, an evaluative approach is needed. This is when the analysis of the video must be done in relation to previously determined criteria, as when rating a teaching according to a set of criteria. Examples where this might occur include fidelity coaching for a new math professional learning program, submission of video for the purposes of teacher licensure, or routine assessment of teaching in student teaching or among in-service teachers. Analyzing video in relation to a checklist, rubric, or other set of criteria also takes place among supervisors, administrators, or coaches who need to norm their scores on observation rubrics and develop a shared professional vision. "*Learning how I look in relation to set criteria*" is an important short- and long-term goal for teachers who wish to be on the same page with school-, district-, and research-based improvement initiatives.

WHAT ARE CONSIDERATIONS IN THE DESIGN OF VIDEO-BASED TASKS FOR TEACHER LEARNING?

Implementing video analysis across the teacher-learning continuum depends on thoughtful task design. In their review of the use of video in professional learning for teachers, Blomberg, Seidel, Renkl, Sherin, and Borko (2013) identified five considerations that inform instructional choices that facilitators must make when designing video analysis tasks. These are adapted and expanded below and are built upon throughout the design of the following chapters.

Designing Video-Based Teacher Professional Learning: Five Considerations

1. **Consider the stage of teacher learning you/your participants are at and the learning goals you seek for yourself/them.** For instance, are teachers just beginning to look at their practice, or have they been involved in other observation experiences, like learning walks, in the past?

   → *What are the goals for teacher learning in this experience?*

2. **Choose video analysis as a tool only where appropriate.** For example, is video essential to achieve your goals for teacher learning, or is reviewing student work samples or engaging in curriculum development more relevant?

   → *How does video analysis support your teacher-learning goals?*

3. **Review the learning goals and instructional strategies you have set forth for teacher learning and determine which kind of video materials would best suit the task, as each kind has different strengths.**

   → *Which type of video fits the task you have designed for your teachers—video of self? Video of colleagues? Video of unknown others? Which video materials and of what length best suit the tasks?*

4. **Recognize that some video tasks present particular challenges, such as availability, comfort level, and accessibility.** For instance, some video tasks require teachers who are ready to video their own practice while others can work with videos from online sources. Sometimes the subject area or student profile can make it harder to find appropriate video.

   → *How is the design of the video analysis task made accessible and barrier-free to teacher participants?*

5. **Assess teacher learning in ways that reflect the skills developed.** For instance, if you are hoping to develop descriptive versus evaluative observation skills, then asking teachers to "rate" performance on a video of teaching goes against the skills that were developed in the task.

   → *How can teacher learning be assessed using video-based tasks that parallel the video analysis activities that are part of the professional learning experience?*

WHAT ARE THE PRIMARY APPROACHES FOR ENGAGING TEACHERS IN VIDEO ANALYSIS?

In examining hundreds of research articles on video analysis, Baecher, Kung, Ward, and Kern (2018) found seven modes were primarily used to engage teachers. While they vary from being more closed ended to more open ended, they each provide the teacher participant with concrete steps to follow and are led by a process and a facilitator. This is vital for the success of video analysis for teacher learning.

1. *Group Discussion*

   - This involves groups of teachers coming together to discuss video records of practice with the purpose of advancing their noticing skills, for a particular purpose or to deepen methodological understandings, often called "Video Clubs" (van Es, 2012) or "Video Learning Communities" (Baecher, Rorimer, & Smith, 2012). For example, Brantlinger, Sherin, and Linsenmeier (2011) describe a series of 16 weekly meetings among mathematics teachers preparing for National Board Certification, who focused on their work fostering classroom discourse.

2. *Structured Viewing Guides*

   - In these studies, a series of prompt questions was provided to teachers in order to help guide their viewing of video, either their own or that of others. These were usually completed by teachers on their own, prior to meeting with peers, a supervisor, or the researcher. One example is from Deaton (2012), who uses a viewing guide to facilitate elementary-level science teachers' examination of critical incidents in their lessons, using her provided reflective framework.

3. *Reflective Writing*

   - More extensive than the shorter responses required from structured viewing guides, reflective writing involved participants in either regular or elaborated writing as a way to process teachers' thoughts about seeing their practice on video. For instance, Payant's (2014) study of TESOL teacher candidates employed reflective writing as a facilitative process to draw out their reflections on practice, identity, and lesson design as they reviewed videos from micro-teaching episodes.

4. *One-on-One Reflective Learning Conversations*

   - These studies are characterized by their use of conversations, usually between a supervisor or coach, to facilitate teachers' reflection on a lesson they have taught. Studies such as Sydnor's (2016) explore the impact of a supervisory conference held when video is utilized to support dialogic, collaborative talk.

5. *Online Video Annotation*

   - These studies supported teachers' observations of their own and other lessons via interactive programs designed for online review. These programs were designed by the authors and usually involved features such as timestamping, comment boxes, and guiding checklists. Colasante (2011) shares such a media annotation tool (MAT), which facilitated reflection on teaching and assessment activities of physical education preservice teachers' course.

6. *Observation Rubric*

   - These studies utilized a widely known observation tool or created one for the purposes of their contexts and asked teachers to carefully review video of practice and rate the teaching in the video—their own or others'—according to the criteria on the provided rubric. An example is La Paro, Maynard, Thomason, and Scott-Little's (2012) study of early childhood educators' video reflections guided by Pianta, La Paro, and Hamre's (2006) classroom assessment scoring system (CLASS).

7. *Discourse Analysis*

- This involves teachers transcribing the speech that took place in the video clip and carefully segmenting it in terms of some guiding framework. For instance, Schieble, Vetter, and Meacham (2015) describe how a preservice teacher used discourse analysis to critically reflect on how positions of power affect teacher identities.

The modes described above directly relate to the purpose of this book—which is to provide clear facilitation guidelines for video analysis in teacher learning. Each of these modes will appear in the suggested video analysis activities presented in the chapters in the second half of this text. Being more explicit about facilitation moves can benefit teacher educators, school leaders, coaches, and all who work to support teacher learning. In other words, there is a wide research base and strong evidence for the potential for video to impact teacher thinking and behavior. However, very few of these studies offer specific, step-by-step guidelines for a classroom educator to replicate or approximate the processes involved. This text is designed to provide a needed link to the robust and continuously emerging, relatively recent body of research that has examined the impact of video analysis on professional learning.

The following chapters are structured to provide a review of essential skills and conditions for successful implementation of video analysis tasks for teacher learning. These are presented in Chapters 2 and 3. In Chapter 4, a discussion of the technical considerations for producing teacher video is provided, as that is often a concern early on in the process. Chapters 5 through 9 offer progressively more challenging video analysis tasks in a detailed, practical manner with a facilitator-user in mind. Chapter 10 addresses the development of a video library and how to access video that is readily available online. The conclusion situates video analysis in the teacher education and school contexts, based on how it has been used in various settings and by educators in various roles.

PUTTING IDEAS INTO ACTION

Revisiting the scenarios presented at the start of this chapter, what do you now see as valuable—even essential—for the introduction of video into teacher learning?

1. What experiences have you had being observed with or without video? How do you imagine the experience as well as the learning outcomes might be affected by the introduction of video analysis into the process?

2. At what stages are the teachers you work with, and which type of video analysis tasks do you envision being useful to them?

3. How might the suggestions for designing video analysis tasks assist you in your planning for the use of video, or which have you already utilized?

4. What types of facilitation approaches have you experienced or used with teachers? Which appeal to you?

5. Which parts of this chapter resonate for you in terms of facilitating other teachers' conversations or for your own use of video analysis?

Chapter References

Alexander, M., Williams, N. A., & Nelson, K. L. (2012). When you can't get there: Using video self-monitoring as a tool for changing the behaviors of pre-service teachers. *Rural Special Education Quarterly, 31*(4), 18–24.

Baecher, L., Kung, S. C., Jewkes, A. M., & Rosalia, C. (2013). The role of video for self-evaluation in early field experiences. *Teaching and Teacher Education, 36*, 189–197.

Baecher, L., Kung, S. K., Ward, S., & Kern, K. (2018). Facilitating video analysis for teacher development: A systematic review of the research. *Journal of Technology and Teacher Education, 26*(2), 185–216.

Baecher, L., & McCormack, B. (2015). The impact of video review on supervisory conferencing. *Language and Education, 29*(2), 153–173.

Baecher, L., Rorimer, S., & Smith, L. (2012). Video-mediated teacher collaborative inquiry: Focus on English language learners. *The High School Journal, 95*(3), 49–61.

Blomberg, G., Seidel, T., Renkl, A., Sherin, M. G., & Borko, H. (2013). Five research-based heuristics for using video in pre-service teacher education. *Journal for Educational Research Online/Journal Für Bildungsforschung Online, 5*(1), 90–114.

Brantlinger, A., Sherin, M. G., & Linsenmeier, K. A. (2011). Discussing discussion: A video club in the service of math teachers' National Board preparation. *Teachers and Teaching: Theory and Practice, 17*(1), 5–33.

Colasante, M. (2011). Using video annotation to reflect on and evaluate physical education pre-service teaching practice. *Australasian Journal of Educational Technology, 27*(1), 66–88.

Deaton, C. (2012). Examining the use of a reflection framework to guide teachers' video analysis of their science teaching practice. *European Journal of Science Education, 16*(2), 1–21.

Fukkink, R. G., Trienekens, N., & Kramer, L. J. (2011). Video feedback in education and training:

Putting learning in the picture. *Educational Psychology Review, 23*(1), 45–63.

Goldman-Segall, R. (1995). Configurational validity: A proposal for analyzing ethnographic multimedia narratives. *Journal of Educational Multimedia and Hypermedia, 4*, 163–182.

Grossman, P. (2010). *Learning to practice: The design of clinical experience in teacher preparation* (Policy Brief). Washington, DC: American Association of Colleges of Teacher Education.

La Paro, K. M., Maynard, C., Thomason, A., & Scott-Little, C. (2012). Developing teachers' classroom interactions: A description of a video review process for early childhood education students. *Journal of Early Childhood Teacher Education, 33*(3), 224–238.

Marsh, B., & Mitchell, N. (2014). The role of video in teacher professional development. *Teacher Development, 18*(3), 403–417.

Nagro, S. S., & Cornelius, K. E. (2013). Evaluating the evidence base of video analysis. *Teacher Education and Special Education, 36*(4), 312–329.

Orland-Barak, L., & Maskit, D. (2017). Video as 'Observing Experience.' In *Methodologies of mediation in professional learning* (pp. 51–62). Cham, Switzerland: Springer International Publishing.

Payant, C. (2014). Incorporating video-mediated reflective tasks in MATESOL programs. *TESL Canada Journal, 31*(2), 1–21.

Pianta, R. C., La Paro, K. M., & Hamre, B. K. (2006). *Classroom Assessment Scoring System* [CLASS]. Charlottesville, VA: University of Virginia.

Rosaen, C. L., Lundeberg, M., Cooper, M., Fritzen, A., & Terpstra, M. (2008). Noticing noticing: How does investigation of video records change how teachers reflect on their experiences? *Journal of Teacher Education, 59*(4), 347–360.

Schieble, M., Vetter, A., & Meacham, M. (2015). A discourse analytic approach to video analysis of teaching: Aligning desired identities with practice. *Journal of Teacher Education, 66*(3), 245–260.

Sydnor, J. (2016). Using video to enhance reflective practice: Student teachers' dialogic examination of their own teaching. *The New Educator*, *12*(1), 67–84.

Tripp, T., & Rich, P. (2012). Using video to analyze one's own teaching. *British Journal of Educational Technology*, *43*(4), 678–704.

van Es, E. A. (2012). Using video to collaborate around problems of practice. *Teacher Education Quarterly*, *39*(2), 103–116.

Yadav, A., & Koehler, M. (2007). The role of epistemological beliefs in preservice teachers' interpretation of video cases of early-grade literacy instruction. *Journal of Technology and Teacher Education*, *15*(3), 335–361.

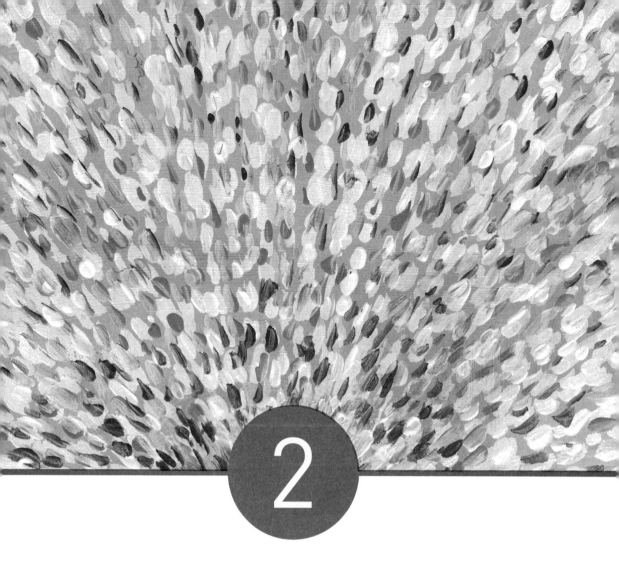

2

WHAT OBSERVATION SKILLS NEED TO BE IN PLACE BEFORE I GET STARTED WITH VIDEO?

Until you make the unconscious conscious, it will direct your life and you will call it fate.

—Carl Jung

Look at this image carefully and then jot down three observations.

1. _____

   _____

2. _____

   _____

3. _____

   _____

https://istock.com/diane555

Perhaps you wrote something about a boy running to catch the school bus, the boy wearing a t-shirt, and the boy being late to school. Now, take a look at the statements you wrote down. Which are descriptive? Which are evaluative? Reviewing the three statements above, for example, only one is descriptive: "The boy is wearing a t-shirt." Assuming that the boy is running to catch the bus or that he is late for school are inferences. It could well be that he is simply out for a run at the same time a school bus happens to be passing by.

In this chapter, a framework for how our brain processes input and forms opinions is shared, followed by several considerations for supporting teachers' building of classroom observation skills through nonjudgmental, descriptive note-taking. These ways of approaching observation lay the foundation for a mindset that helps teachers appreciate their classroom as a research stage full of many possible interpretations and to become consciously able to distinguish evaluation, evidence, and description. While the principles of this chapter can be applied to live classroom observations, the steps are also essential to foster readiness for video analysis of teaching.

THE PSYCHOLOGY OF JUDGMENT

The human brain is wired to quickly survey the landscape and formulate quick judgments—these are instinctual, survival skills. However, when it comes to classroom observation, we must consciously learn to keep those fast judgments at bay, in essence circumventing our natural wiring. This makes classroom observation really challenging and even trying at times.

Kahneman, author of *Thinking, Fast and Slow* (2011), was awarded the Nobel Prize for his seminal work in psychology that explains the two systems that drive the way we think. The descriptions of the functions of these two systems clarify why it is we jump to conclusions when we observe and also how we are capable of overcoming these snap judgments.

SYSTEMS FOR THINKING

System 1

- Quick, automatic and intuitive

- Relies on feelings and instincts

- Instantly evaluates events and sends impressions to System 2

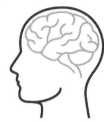

https://istock.com/ruthyoel

System 2

- Slow, requires conscious attention

- Deliberates and considers evidence

- Receives impressions from System 1 and usually turns them into beliefs

Recognizing the existence of these two systems sheds light on the example at the beginning of this chapter. We see a man running next to a bus, and we quickly evaluate the situation and conclude that he is late for work. Looking at the same scene with our "System 2" brain, we would carefully describe everything we see in the picture and then deliberate on the evidence. Imagining the scene were of a classroom interaction and not a man running next to a bus, we can see that the System 1 way of observing may lead us to some erroneous conclusions, whereas the System 2 process could slow us down and require us to challenge our initial impressions.

One of the biggest dangers in classroom observation from our System 1 thinking is bias. When System 1 is doing our thinking, we are not aware of our own processes, and that is where ableist, sexist, racist, classist and other preexisting beliefs take hold without our even being aware they are in operation. In other words, our implicit biases become explicit actions that can impede student growth (Staats, Capatosto, Tenney, & Mamo, 2017). We have to always assume those are present, just beyond our consciousness. Therefore, we must take those measures needed to move into System 2 very deliberately, even when it feels painstaking and time consuming to do so because the way we think directly impact the ways we treat students.

For instance, these implicit biases manifest into behaviors such as believing Asian students will be high achievers, treating students with physical abilities as if they have an intellectual disability, or assuming students with accents need writing help. *Project Implicit* at Harvard University has a variety of free self-assessment tools for teachers to engage in a discovery process about their implicit biases (https://implicit.harvard.edu/implicit/selectatest.html). Having honest conversations about bias is essential before engaging in classroom observation. Otherwise, we run the risk that what we "observe" is more of a projection of our beliefs than a reflection of the evidence.

LEARNING TO LOOK DELIBERATELY IN CLASSROOM OBSERVATION

When considering video as a tool in teacher professional learning, it is important to first establish a strong rationale for observing classrooms. Some of the benefits of learning to observe more deliberately include the following:

"

In the classroom, where there's so much going on, it's easy to be on autopilot, moving from one child to another, one place to the next, scanning the room just to be sure everything's okay. But when you slow down just a little bit, you can see and hear so much more (Jablon, 2010, p. 24).

- Gathering evidence toward meeting learning targets

- Assessing the impact of methods, techniques, and curricula

- Reflecting on the connection between teaching and learning

- Identifying students' strengths

- Challenging one's implicit biases

- Getting to know how students learn, which increases their sense of trust and the teacher's ability to meet their needs

- Addressing dilemmas by slowing down System 1 reactions and taking more time to thoughtfully respond rather than react

After a discussion about bias has taken place and possibly some self-assessments for this bias as well, facilitators of teacher learning may want to explore four closely inter-related concepts in classroom observation:

1. *What we see is different from what we intentionally observe.*

2. *What we see is partial.*

3. *What we see can be seen differently from other perspectives.*

4. *What we see we make inferences about.*

1. ***What we see is different from what we intentionally observe.*** When carrying out observations of classrooms, we tend to believe what we are seeing is a result of conscious attention. Most times, however, what we "see" or "notice" is done through lenses we are not aware of, as was discussed earlier in terms of implicit bias and the immediate functioning of our System 1 processes. The following activity can get teachers talking about this concept, using a photo of a busy classroom scene.

Seeing Versus Observing

1. Round 1: Ask teachers to examine a photo of a classroom and simply write down all the things they see in the image within a two-minute period of time.

https://iStock.com/SolStock

2. Have teachers form pairs and compare their lists. Teachers can then discuss questions such as the following:

   • Are your lists identical? Why not?

   • How challenging did you find it to write down everything you saw in the image in the short-time period? Is it possible to see everything?

   • What does this task suggest about doing classroom observation?

3. Round 2: Ask teachers to then look at the picture again, but this time to only write down what they see related to materials. What materials do they see in use in this image? Ask them to write down everything they see with this focus, for two minutes.

4. Teachers can then form pairs and again compare their lists. Teachers can then discuss questions such as the following:

   • Are your lists identical? Why or why not?

   • How challenging did you find it to write down everything you saw in the image in the short-time period during this round? How was it different from the first round?

   • What does this task suggest about doing classroom observation?

Seeing Versus Observing can be a way to begin the awareness process of how different it is to be intentional when we notice classroom behaviors. Like putting blinders on a horse, we gain focus when we restrict ourselves from distracting additional visual information.

2. ***What we see is partial.*** In the Seeing Versus Observing activity above, we gathered more information when we focused on just one aspect of the classroom image, but of course there is much we do *not* see because of that narrowed focus. Partial viewing will always take place, resulting from the biases we hold, the angle we are viewing, or even just the fact that we simply glance away and miss certain events.

Another reason we only see "partially" is that when we are visually presented with many factors, we utilize preexisting expectations to discount distractors. This explains why we can observe more when we are told to focus on a particular viewing target—as opposed to seeing everything in a scene. This is due to the way our System 1 thinking copes with the extensive visual information we are presented with and results in our inability to see objects that we do not expect to see. This was demonstrated in a well-known experiment in which viewers are told to watch a video of two teams playing basketball and count how many times the basketball is passed back and forth. A second video of a girl walking by with an umbrella is superimposed on the basketball scene. Almost 80% of viewers fail to notice the girl with the umbrella.

> In the years since, hundreds of studies have backed up the idea that when attention is occupied with one thing, people often fail to notice other things right before their eyes . . . we are constantly overlooking much of the world around us and no, there is nothing mysterious about it. The key is to realize that this is just what attention is: selectivity. For a brain with finite computing power, zooming in to focus on one thing always means picking up less information about everything else. (Payne, 2013)

Another brief activity can be used to explore this concept. In this well-known image, used by psychologist Edgar Rubin in 1915, two faces can be seen in profile but if looked at in a different way, a vase is seen. It is virtually impossible to "see" both the vase and the faces at the same time, but we are able to shift back and forth between those views once the alternate is pointed out to us.

Two Sides of the Same Coin

1. Ask teachers to examine this image for 10 seconds and write down what they see.

2. Have teachers form pairs and compare what they saw. Sometimes, some can see both or only one or the other. Pairs should help anyone who is not able to see both images. Teachers can be invited to consider this image and discuss how it can serve as a metaphor for classroom observation.

   • Are you able to see both the vase and the faces? Does it get easier, and if so, why do you think that is the case?

https://pixabay.com/ElisaRiva

   • How does this image relate to the idea that we only see partially when we observe?

   • What could we keep in mind from this activity—now that we realize there is an alternate "reality" always possible within the scenes we observe?

Two Sides of the Same Coin can further the awareness process of how limited, one sided, and partial our views of classroom situations may well be. The takeaway is to be humble about our observations with the knowledge that there is always information we are not perceiving.

3. *What we see can be seen differently from other perspectives.*

A natural corollary to the notion that what we see may not be what others see is that there are many perspectives on any given situation under observation. These points of view are both enriched and constrained by the limits of our prior knowledge and experience. This means that, when we are observing, what we repeatedly notice is based on our backgrounds. "My experience is what I agree to attend to. Only those items which I notice shape my mind" (James, 1950). As the quote suggests, our knowledge building is confined to what we notice, and what we notice continually reinforces what we know.

If we ask teachers to return to the classroom image featured in the Seeing Versus Observing activity, they can recall that the lists they created were not identical. Teachers from different backgrounds noticed different aspects of classrooms and bring different "lenses" to their viewing. These lenses can be subconscious, stemming from bias, or conscious, arising from our knowledge base and experience. From the Two Sides of the Same Coin, we know that there are likely other lenses that could also be valid—lenses we do not have or do not yet have. The following activity explores how we see different features when we look with different points of view on the same scene.

Looking With Different Lenses

1. Ask teachers to examine the same or a new photo of a classroom or a short video clip of teaching and write down all the things they see in the image within a two-minute period of time. It can be interesting to utilize classroom images from unfamiliar settings, as these can trigger bias, personal beliefs, and judgments (e.g., https://www.theguardian.com/world/gallery/2015/oct/02/schools-around-the-world-un-world-teachers-day-in-pictures or https://www.learner.org/libraries/tfl/chinese/gao/analyze.html at 16:30 for two minutes), which makes the activity even more revealing in terms of our "lenses." Adapting Brookfield's (2017) approach to reflection, which is based on purposefully taking up different vantage points or "lenses," invite teachers to look and relook at the same image (or video) but with different points of view.

Viewing Lens	Individual Notes	Question to Share With a Partner or Group
Autobiographical lens: Examine the image in relation to your own experiences as a student or teacher. Write down what you see through this lens.	Notes:	Are your lists identical? In what ways do they reflect your personal or professional background knowledge—in other words, how does your "autobiographical lens" shape what you notice?
Student lens: Try to put yourself in your students' shoes and review the image by looking at what is happening through their eyes.	Notes:	How might students perceive the same image? How does adopting a "student lens" shape what you notice?

(Continued)

(Continued)

Viewing Lens	Individual Notes	Question to Share With a Partner or Group
Look at the scene from the perspective of • An early childhood educator • A special educator • An English as a second language educator • A school administrator, and so forth	Notes:	How does taking up these different perspectives offer new insights? Do they provide competing or complementary information?

2. Teachers can share their findings and what they gained from trying out various lenses as they observed. Teachers can then discuss questions such as the following:

   • What professional lenses do we believe we view classroom practice through?
   • How might intentionally adopting different points of view enrich the data gained in classroom observation?
   • What does this task suggest about doing classroom observation?

In Horowitz's (2013) *On Looking: Eleven Walks With Expert Eyes*, she describes her experiment of taking a walk around her familiar city block with eleven different experts. Each companion—an artist, a geologist, a physician, a sociologist, and so forth—sees the world in unique ways, bringing a particular expertise and "lens." This, like the activity "Looking With Different Lenses," reminds us that human attention and perception color what our minds determine to be salient. Therefore, we can only see what we know to look for. If we are not yet trained in looking at methods in second language teaching, for example, we are not able to see those aspects in practice. The task can add another layer of caution to prevent us from jumping to the conclusion that what we see is what everyone sees.

4. *What we see we make inferences about.*

Another tricky aspect to observation is closely related to the previous ideas; when we observe, we cannot help but make inferences about what we are seeing. Inferencing is a natural System 1 thinking process, resulting from the brain's desire to arrive at quick, global assessments rather than waste valuable memory on all the details that surround us. Like the optical illusion in the photograph below, our minds register very quickly and only when startled, surprised, or required to, go back to engage with System 2 processing to better understand what we see.

In the classic *Drawing on the Right Side of the Brain*, Edwards (2012) has shown aspiring artists that rapid improvement in the realism in our drawings can be achieved when we stop drawing our symbolic, redacted ideas of what we expect a thing is supposed to look like and instead learn to look at the actual shapes, proportions, relationships, shadows, and light that form an object.

Like the artist learning to look at the parts rather than superimposing a preconception, looking carefully in classroom observation without "filling in the gaps" can improve our skills. Even when we believe we are aware of our biases, particular perspectives, and how our backgrounds impact what is salient to us, when we try to objectively describe what we are seeing, our brains are busily making inferences that lead to conclusions. We then note those conclusions down as observation data, but they are data with a high amount of inferencing. Learning to take low-inference notes is an active move to build awareness of the four concepts presented here about classroom observation and can be begun with a simple activity, followed by elaborated work on low-inference note-taking.

A Coppery Object

1. Hand out a penny to each set of partner teachers. Make sure that the pennies vary in color and age.

2. Ask the partners to come up with 10 observations of their "object." Do not use the word "penny" in the instructions.

3. Have the pairs look at their lists and decide which observations were judgments and which were descriptions.

4. Ask the teachers to share out their observations. As each is read aloud, consider if they require inference. For example, challenge statements like "*It's a penny*" and "*Lincoln is on the front*"—do they require inference? If I were from (name a country no one has heard of), would I know this object is a penny? Would I know it is Lincoln? How could I change the observation to make it lower inference (e.g., "It is a man in profile")? Share the idea that if the statement does require background or prior knowledge, it is *high inference*. If I call it "shiny" or "dirty," is this a judgment call? If so, these statements are high inference. Ones that are purely descriptive are *low-inference*.

5. After reviewing the observation statements and determining whether they are high or low inference, questions can be raised like the following:

   • What is a definition of high versus low inference you could create?

   • Why is it important to think about inferences we are making when we observe?

   • In what ways do low-inference statements provide information that high-inference statements do not?

   • How did you feel when some of the observations were rejected for being high inference?

   • What is a takeaway for classroom observation?

Low-Inference Classroom Obs,

Collecting low-inference evidence in the form of notes during an observation works toward ensuring that what the observer is recording would be equally observable by others (reliable) and is a true description of events as they occurred (valid). Low inference note-taking reduces bias because it captures specific actions and statements rather than being interpretive (Archer et al., 2016). When we receive feedback from observers that is not reliable and lacks validity, we cannot engage in authentic reflection for improvement. However, as a result of all the nuances mentioned in this chapter, which are inherent in observation, it is important to stress that low-inference classroom observation is very challenging. It is essential, however, for it allows us to

- Dramatically increase practitioners' capacity to accurately observe practice

- Engage in collegial conversations about a classroom event without debating the facts

- Illuminate small changes in practice across classrooms that make a big difference in learning

- Identify patterns within and across classrooms to inform more targeted professional learning (Barge, 2013)

Working toward low-inference classroom observation intentionally, with frequent checks, is part of the process. Teachers can begin by developing or reviewing a list of characteristics of low-inference observation notes, such as presented in the following chart:

Low-Inference Notes	High-Inference Notes
• Record only what is observable.	• Record beyond what is observable.
• Contain descriptive language.	• Contain evaluative language.
• Use specifics.	• Use generalizations.
• Use exact counts "5 students."	• Use vague quantifiers "A lot of."
• Begin with "I see," or "I hear."	• Begin with "I think," or "I feel."
• Use jargon-free descriptors "The teacher showed a picture of a zoo."	• Use education jargon "the teacher differentiated."
• Provide facts, descriptions.	• Provide opinions, conclusions, judgments.
• Praise and advice free.	• Contain praise and advice.

High or Low?

1. Use available samples, such as these which are adapted from the Newark, New Jersey, school district (http://www.nps.k12.nj.us/wp-content/uploads/sites/111/2014/09/highinferencevslowinferenceobservationexamples.pdf).

2. Invite teachers to read the way the statements are worded in the low- and the high-inference columns. Consider the following:

- How are the statements different? How do they fit the definitions provided in the previous chart?
- How might the teacher feel hearing the high-inference version versus the low-inference version during a post-observation conference?
- Which do you think provide more data for the teacher's growth?

Low-Inference Notes	High-Inference Notes
• Four students finished the Do Now with time to spare and then engaged in conversation. Five minutes passed, and then the teacher began reviewing the Do Now.	• The lesson pace was too slow.
• When teacher was reviewing the answers on the homework, student responders provided their answers. The teacher did not ask students to explain how they arrived at their answers.	• You did not demand precision and evidence in student responses.
• It took forty seconds to pass out the journal prompt worksheets after rug time. Teacher-assigned student journal captains distributed the sheets.	• Routines were tight and maximized instructional time.
• Teacher called on 7 out of 23 students to give the answers between 10:15 and 10:20.	• Teacher checked for student understanding for some of the class but not all.

3. Another step is to provide statements like the ones above, cut into strips, and to have teachers sort them into low- or high-inference notes. Questions can then be posed such as the following:

- How can you tell whether the statement is low or high inference?
- How could you change the high-inference statement into a low-inference one?
- How does taking low-inference notes change the way you might observe?
- Which kind of notes would you prefer an observer to take?

AWARENESS OF JUDGMENT IN THE OBSERVATION PROCESS

After participating in these kinds of awareness-building activities related to observation, teachers may feel almost afraid to make any claims or very hesitant about making statements. This is actually a positive—for being cautious and careful about the observations we make sparks our System 2 thinking and encourages us to review evidence and corroborate our findings. This is where video records can be so helpful, for they offer the opportunity to examine classroom interactions with others and in a slowed-down way that allows for us to question our initial assumptions and quick evaluations.

At the same time, it is important to situate classroom observation within the field of scientific inquiry and acknowledge that expertise is valuable, as observation skills also *do* depend on making connections to prior knowledge.

> The thing noticed will only become significant if the mind of the observer either consciously or unconsciously relates it to some relevant knowledge or past experience, or if in pondering on it subsequently he arrives at some hypothesis . . . one cannot observe everything closely, therefore one must discriminate and try to select the significant . . . the "trained" observer deliberately looks for specific things which his training has taught him are significant. (Beveridge, 2017, p. 98)

This quote presents the core tension in nonjudgmental, descriptive classroom observation. How does one simultaneously observe as objectively as possible (being cautious and aware of preexisting biases, stepping back from evaluating, understanding the limitations of one's background on what one can see, and scrupulously avoiding inferences), while also logically building upon extensive research findings and determining what to attend to that is likely to be significant?

KEY FOCI IN CLASSROOM OBSERVATION

One way to handle these competing notions—that we best observe without preconceptions but that we also observe best by discrimination based on expertise—is to become aware of and harness both aspects of the process. Using a pre/while/post approach to classroom observation can be a useful tool.

PRE-OBSERVATION

Use your background knowledge, area of expertise, teachers' interests, colleagues with experience, and research findings to narrow a focus for observation. The lists below provide suggestions for generic foci as well as of discipline-specific foci. All of these are included because they have been linked to positive results in students' academic performance in U.S. classrooms (e.g., the CLASS; https://curry.virginia.edu/classroom-assessment-scoring-system). Foci should be selected in advance of the observation based on teacher interest, student need, prior-observation feedback, professional-learning priorities, and so forth. Some foci are better explored by looking at lesson plans or by examining student work rather than classroom observation. To determine whether a focus could work for classroom observation, consider four questions:

1. Is this a focus strongly connected to student outcomes?

2. Can I "see" this focal area while I observe the lesson or would I be inferring it?

3. Can I collect descriptive notes on this focus area while I watch the lesson?

4. What would I actually be looking at/ looking for in terms of visible/ audible data for this focus?

For those focus areas that can be well explored via classroom observation, the following lists of topics can be of use. The first is "generic" in that it could be used in most classroom situations, whereas the second list is tied to specific discipline areas.

General Foci for Classroom Observation	
1. Creating an effective environment for student learning	<ul><li>Physical environment</li><li>Routines</li><li>Time management</li><li>Verbal/nonverbal cues</li><li>Teacher affect</li><li>Teacher/student interactions</li><li>Use of praise</li><li>Dealing with disruption</li><li>Giving instructions</li><li>Promoting respect</li><li>Language modeling</li></ul>
2. Planning learning experiences	<ul><li>Setting meaningful objectives</li><li>Accuracy and depth of subject matter explanations</li><li>Connecting to prior knowledge</li><li>Modeling</li><li>Creating access to content</li><li>Sequencing of tasks</li><li>Selection/use of technology</li><li>Selection/use of materials</li><li>Critical thinking activities</li><li>Learner autonomy</li></ul>
3. Engaging all students in learning	<ul><li>Student productivity</li><li>Time on task</li><li>Response opportunities</li><li>Teacher talk versus student talk</li><li>Student-posed questions or student-initiated discussion</li><li>Wait time</li><li>Movement patterns</li><li>Scaffolding</li><li>Differentiation of tasks</li></ul>

(Continued)

(Continued)

General Foci for Classroom Observation	
4. Assessing impact on student learning	• Providing feedback • Questioning • Circulating • Responding to student contributions • Checking for understanding • Involving students in self-assessment • Error correction

The Massachusetts Department of Elementary and Secondary Education has recently developed a series of *What to Look for Observation Guides* across the grades and many subject areas that could be very useful to determine a focus area, particularly when one does not have expertise or experience in the grade level or subject matter: http://www.doe.mass.edu/candi/observation/. The list below is a sample of what such a set of foci might look like when approaching classroom observation through a disciplinary lens.

Sample Discipline-Specific Foci for Classroom Observation	
Early Childhood Education	• Teachers respond to children's negative emotions (hurt, fear, anger) by offering comfort, support, and assistance. • Teacher transitions students across classroom spaces efficiently. • Teachers use words that children may not understand and provide explanations or examples of these words. • Students are using newly learned language when speaking. • Students are working cooperatively on a shared activity. (Adapted from the *NAEYC Class Observation Tool*: https://www.naeyc.org/sites/default/files/globally-shared/downloads/PDFs/accreditation/early-learning/CO%20SV%20Item_Sept%202017.pdf)
English Language Arts	• Teacher and students regularly reference specific texts in class discussions and activities. • Teacher explains *how* students can implement learning strategies (i.e., making predictions, revising text, using quotes to support an argument). • Teacher picks up on students' responses and ideas and presses for elaboration and clarification. (Adapted from the *Protocol for Language Arts Teaching Observation* (PLATO): http://platorubric.stanford.edu/index.html)

Sample Discipline-Specific Foci for Classroom Observation	
Mathematics	• Students voice connections between two representations for a mathematical concept. • Students make predictions, estimations, and/or hypotheses and devise means for testing them. • Students are engaged in mathematical thinking (procedural, conceptual, problem-solving, justification). • Students are working to solve a real-world, genuine, problem. (Adapted from https://www.mathedleadership.org/docs/coaching/ ObservationGuide_Tool.pdf and the *Mathematical Quality of Instruction*: http://hub.mspnet.org/media/data/MQI_062410_Summer_Final.pdf?media_000000006941.pdf)
Science	• Students pose questions or reference prior experiences related to the phenomenon or problem in the lesson. • Students create artifacts (written, oral, pictorial, and kinesthetic) of reasoning behind their answers. • Classroom discourse focuses on explicitly expressing and clarifying student reasoning. (Adapted from the *NGSS Lesson Screener*: https://www.nextgenscience.org/resources/equip-rubric-lessons-units-science)
English as a Second Language	• Teacher specifies target English language to be learned (vocabulary, grammar, discourse features). • Teacher provides structured prompts leading to student practice with the target language. • Teacher models the target language and provides feedback on student language error. • Students are simultaneously learning content and developing English language skills. (Adapted from the *edTPA Handbook in English as an Additional Language*: https://scale.stanford.edu/teaching/edtpa)

Whichever focus is selected, it is always important to keep in mind the following:

- Observation is always influenced by the four concepts presented earlier: bias, inference, limitation, and lens.
- No observation system can address every concern.
- Observing will capture aspects of teaching and learning but cannot alone be used as an assessment of the teacher.
- Multiple views and multiple lenses will peel back more and more layers of the complexity of the classroom.

It is recommended to begin with a "generic" focus before moving to discipline-specific ones; although these foci are also intended to be observed in a low-inference, concrete manner, they do depend on deeper subject-area expertise and should first be unpacked and clarified. Most of the sample items above, while taken from research-based and professional association-developed observation rubrics in their respective disciplines, had to be reworded to be more low inference. Often, rubric language is vague, jargon filled, and employs language like "rich," "effective," or "extensive," which are high-inference, subjective terms. Therefore, be prepared to reformat them so they become less evaluative and more of a roadmap shining a light on what would be worthy to hone in on during an observation.

WHILE OBSERVING

This is the phase of the classroom observation cycle that asks us to now step away from the prior knowledge and expertise to our "alien" stance where we consciously and deliberately collect whatever we see. Using a data collection form that keeps the target in front of us but does not have rating scales, rubric language, or other distractors can help us stay in the nonjudgmental, descriptive note-taking mode. The notes we collect should be low inference so that any other observer would be able to record the same data. In this way, the data is reliable and replicable rather than subject to our personal System 1 lenses.

Low · inference field Notes = Reliability (Dependability, Trustworthiness)

The following suggestions may be helpful in staying low inference:

- Begin by recording only what you hear or only what you see.

- Build speed and accuracy by practicing often on observations of less than 5 to 10 minutes.

- Build stamina by practicing for longer and longer periods of time.

- Develop your own shorthand or coding system (T = teacher, S = student, M = materials) and use drawings to represent groups of students or teacher interaction with students.

- Mark the time at transition points that mark parts of the lesson (Do Now, Teacher Modeling, Student Work, Closure).

Keep questions like these in mind:

- What is the teacher doing?

- What are the students doing?

- What are students saying to the teacher? To each other?

- What is the task?

- How much time is spent on the task?

Search for evidence of student learning:

- Sit with one table/group of students and write down the questions asked and answers given by the students in that group.

- Copy down what each student has written on their paper verbatim into your observation notes. Obtain a handout from the teacher, if available, and record the answers directly onto it.

- Select a problem, determine the correct answer, and tally the number of students who have the correct response written on their papers.

- If possible, take pictures of actual student work during the classroom observation.

The data collection tool below is adapted from the New York City Department of Education (https://www.weteachnyc.org/) and the Georgia Department of Education (http://www.ciclt.net/ul/cpresa/lowinferenceclassroomprotocol.pdf). By setting the focus and tracking the movements, talk, and actions you see the teacher and students engaged in, low-inference notes can be generated on the left. Being realistic about how our minds work, a separate column to the right allows us to capture and release those personal reactions, opinions, and judgments, keeping evaluative language as much as possible to the side.

Classroom Observation Notes

Observer: _____ Date: _____

Teacher(s): _____ Class/grade/subject: _____

Amount of time observed:

Focus for the observation:

What do you see and hear the teacher and students doing? Quantify and quote.

LOW-INFERENCE NOTES			HIGH-INFERENCE NOTES
Time	Teacher(s)	Students	Wonderings/Opinions/Reactions

POST-OBSERVATION

After the notes have been written, it is a good idea to stop about five to eight minutes before the end of the period and take a moment to review them right away, before leaving the classroom. This can enable you to do the following:

- Remove any evaluative language from the left hand and place it into the high-inference column.

- Look for samples of student work to include with the observation notes.

- Ask a student or teacher a clarifying question.

- Circulate the room to gather any remaining data about student learning.

- Return to the focus area and make sure there is evidence collected about it.

PUTTING IDEAS INTO ACTION

Without bringing video records of teaching into the equation, how do the ideas presented in this chapter help you think about classroom observation?

1. Which concepts discussed in this chapter resonated with your experience—either as an observer or when being observed?

2. Of the four concepts described that complexify observation—bias, partial view, multiple perspectives, and inferencing—which do you believe are most concerning? What do you think could be done to address these challenges?

3. What do you anticipate the difficulties for implementing low-inference note-taking might be for you personally or in your setting?

4. Which parts of this chapter do you believe are essential to review before engaging in video-based observation?

Chapter References

Archer, J., Cantrell, S., Holtzman, S. L., Joe, J. N., Tocci, C. M., & Wood, J. (2016). *Better feedback for better teaching: A practical guide to improving classroom observations.* San Francisco, CA: Jossey-Bass.

Barge, J. (2013). *Using low inference feedback and conferencing: A school leader's guide for improvement.* Atlanta, GA: State of Georgia Department of Education. Retrieved from http://www.ciclt.net/ul/cpresa/lowinferencefeedbackparticipantsguide.pdf"

Beveridge, W. I. B. (2017). *The art of scientific investigation.* Ankaran, Slovenia: Edizioni Savine.

Brookfield, S. (2017). *Becoming a critically reflective teacher* (2nd ed.). San Francisco, CA: Jossey-Bass.

Edwards, B. (2012). *Drawing on the right side of the brain: The definitive.* London, United Kingdom: Penguin.

Horowitz, A. (2013). *On looking: Eleven walks with expert eyes*. New York, NY: Simon and Schuster.

Jablon, J. (2010). Taking it all in: Observation in the classroom. *Teaching Young Children, 4*(2), 24–27.

James, W. (1950). *The principles of psychology* (Vol. *1*). New York, NY: Dover. (Original work published 1890)

Kahneman, D. (2011). *Thinking, fast and slow* (Vol. 1). New York, NY: Farrar, Straus and Giroux.

Payne, B. K. (2013, June 11). Your hidden censor: What your mind will not let you see. *Scientific American*. Retrieved from https://www.scientificamerican.com/article/your-hidden-censor-what-your-mind-will-not-let-you-see/

Staats, C., Capatosto, K., Tenney, L., & Mamo, S. (2017). *State of the science: Implicit bias review 2017*. Columbus, OH: Kirwan Institute for the Study of Race and Ethnicity.

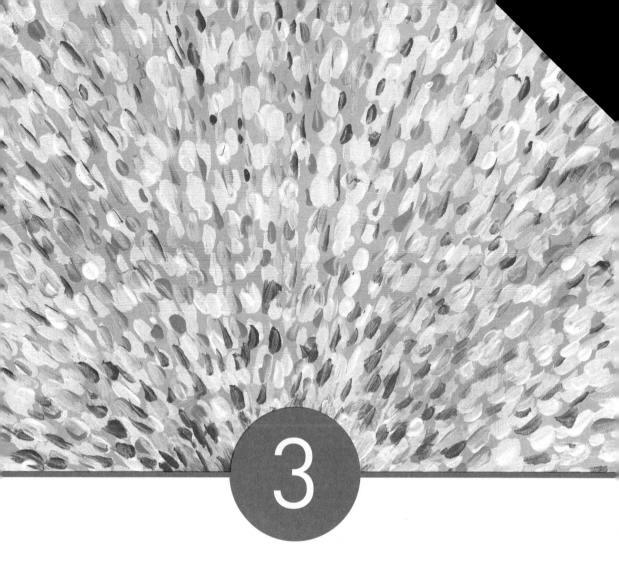

HOW DOES THE WAY WE COMMUNICATE SUPPORT LEARNING WITH VIDEO?

The greatest problem with communication is we don't listen to understand. We listen to reply. When we listen with curiosity, we don't listen with the intent to reply. We listen for what's behind the words.

—Roy T. Bennett, *The Light in the Heart*

CHAPTER OBJECTIVES

- To highlight why video can make teachers feel particularly vulnerable in the learning process
- To present considerations for listening and speaking when engaging in conversations based on video observations
- To identify strategies and communicative moves that maximize the learning for teachers from the video review process.

Marcus and Lizzy sit down to discuss Lizzy's teaching. Lizzy is in her first year of teaching third grade at their school, and Marcus is a peer instructional coach. Marcus has been assigned as Lizzy's mentor. He has visited her classroom frequently, and they have spent time in lesson-planning conversations. Marcus asked Lizzy to record a class that he can't visit because of his busy schedule. Today, they are going to look at some video footage Lizzy has recorded from teaching in this third-grade class.

Marcus starts out by asking her about how the lesson went, and Lizzy speaks of her ongoing struggle with classroom management. Marcus asks her to play some of the video back, and Lizzy asks that it be turned off. "I just can't watch it!" she exclaims. "I don't know where to begin! I am too mortified to look!" Lizzy begins to cry, and Marcus starts reassuring her about what a great job she is doing. She dries her tears, and the session time they have together comes to a close. Lizzy leaves feeling miserable and inadequate, and Marcus does too. Lizzy wonders if she has to keep doing this video-taping of her classes with a feeling of dread, and Marcus wonders what he could have done to make the experience productive for Lizzy rather than defeating.

VIEWING OURSELVES

In spite of the current age of "selfies" and the frequency with which we snap photos, record audio messages, and share videos via our mobile phones and tablets, there is nothing quite as painful as watching oneself teach a lesson on video, as experienced by Lizzy in the vignette above. Why is this so? In Fuller and Manning's (1973) seminal article on the experience of seeing ourselves, they delve into the psychological impact of hearing one's own voice or seeing oneself on video. They note that viewing oneself can cause distress and reactions of fear and anxiety.

> In video and other visual playback, the person's physical self is forcibly brought to his attention. Unless some other focus, perhaps some powerful focus, is provided, self-viewers seem to focus on themselves. . . . Subjects react to voice characteristics, regional accent, a nasal quality, a drawl, whining, head shaking, handwaving. Often the reaction is global.
> "I look awful." "I look better than I thought I would" and so on. Focus on physical manifestations clearly seems to be a part of the self-confrontation experience (pp. 474–475).

At the same time, there is no denying that viewing ourselves captures our attention. Fuller and Manning point to Ronchi and Ripple's (1972) attribution theory as an explanation of this phenomenon. When teachers are in the moment of teaching, they are visually focused on their environment. They believe they are simply responsive in those moments, while they attribute consistent personality characteristics to students and believe these immutable characteristics produce their behavior. When teachers observe themselves on video, the teacher-viewer reacts to the teacher on screen and now attributes behaviors to innate traits as well. This is the first destabilizing effect of video viewing of oneself—attributing traits to ourselves just as we do when we view others. Yet, that person we are viewing and judging is us!

This leads us to consider what our internal intentions, hopes, and beliefs were in the moments we see ourselves acting in contrary ways. This discomfort is the cognitive dissonance that is the second destabilizing aspect of viewing oneself on video. As Fuller and Manning emphasize, the process is psychological as well as intellectual. While viewing oneself increases self-awareness, "It is possible that what many people fear from self-confrontation actually occurs: what they see is different from what they expected and worse than what they hoped for" (p. 476). When we sense that this discomfort might be our experience once we view ourselves, we might go to great lengths to avoid this experience.

Too often, teachers have had negative experiences with supervision and observation. When teachers are accustomed to feeling defensive before a supervisor's observation, anticipating criticism, they bring those feelings to self-observation via video as well. When teachers are experiencing the discomfort of seeing themselves on video and beginning to notice their own automatic behaviors, it is essential to proceed with utmost care and regard. It is really critical not to underestimate how vulnerable teachers may feel once they have video recorded, and especially when asked to share their video. There are a number of ways to lower teachers' stress levels and increase the possibilities of being able to benefit from self-observation.

Ten Tips for Lowering Teachers' Stress about Video-Recording Their Teaching	
	1. Invite teachers to video record strictly on a voluntary basis.
	2. Show teachers how to use their own devices to capture video, so they don't have to worry about new technologies and can control when they want to record.
	3. Ask teachers to video only 5 to 10 minutes and then turn off the camera rather than taping entire lessons.
	4. Offer to assist them with the video-recording process while live observation is already taking place.
	5. Provide teachers with opportunities to video without obligation to share.
	6. Clearly establish that the video records teachers create are their own property, to keep, share, or destroy.
	7. Offer teachers video-editing instruction so that they can isolate and clip out only those portions of video with which they wish to work.

(Continued)

(Continued)

8. Guide teachers to employ purely descriptive commentary through the use of tallies, transcribing, and other observation methods that short-circuit judgment-making.

9. As a group leader, show your video first before asking participants to share theirs.

10. Provide teachers a chance to practice looking at other teachers' videos whom they don't know, either from online sources or other available materials, to practice non-evaluative observation so they can transfer those habits to their own viewing.

TALKING ABOUT TEACHERS' VIDEOS

Chapter 1 reviewed some core considerations for those who plan to design video-based teacher professional learning, and Chapter 2 introduced some ways that teachers can approach classroom observation with a descriptive rather than evaluative mindset. These nonjudgmental ways of looking are the groundwork for teachers to then move to examination of their own practice. Once teachers have created video footage that they are ready to discuss, it is essential that some guidelines for these discussions are introduced and reviewed, whether the conversation is to take place between peer teachers in pairs, in groups, or with supervisors.

INTENTIONAL LISTENING

Although much emphasis in conversations is placed on what the teacher is to say about their video, it is just as important to consider the role of the conversational partner as an attentive and careful listener. Brenda Ueland (1993), in her thoughtful reflection on what it is to be a listener, puts it thus:

> Listening is a magnetic and strange thing, a creative force. Think how the friends that really listen to us are the ones we move toward, and we want to sit in their radius as though it did us good, like ultraviolet rays. This is the reason: When we are listened to, it creates us, makes us unfold and expand. Ideas actually begin to grow within us and come to life. (p. 2)

To Listen

Ear —

聽

> Virtue
> - Heart
> - Eyes
> - Undivided attention

However, in spite of best intentions and a good deal of courage as they prepare to share their videos, there are several unproductive habits that educators can fall into when beginning a conversation with other teachers about their videos. Naming these can be very helpful before asking teachers to converse, as by recognizing common listening missteps and the good intentions behind them, teachers can be more deliberate about how they will engage.

EIGHT CONSIDERATIONS
FOR INTENTIONAL LISTENING

1. **Beware of hijacking the talk**.

   Samantha and Jerry sit down to discuss Jerry's video. He begins by pointing out that he has trouble keeping the opening of the lesson down to just a few minutes before engaging the students in group work. Samantha interjects, "Oh, that same thing always happens to me . . ." and continues to share how she has noticed she also runs into this problem. Pretty soon Jerry is listening to Samantha talk about her teaching and the video is not played any further.

   → To ease the discomfort teachers experience when sharing their videos, listeners may rush to sympathize and, in so doing, turn the focus of the talk back to themselves rather than allowing the teacher's concern to stay as the focus. Instead of conveying to Jerry that she is very understanding of the situation, as Samantha means to, she actually turns the conversation to herself, and he winds up in the listener role. This conversational narcissism can also be a habit of the listener, who has a strong desire to discuss him/herself and treats the conversational partner more as a mirror or a receptacle for his/her own talk. Establishing new norms of interaction can be difficult for some but essential for fostering collaborative conversations (Kochan & Trimble, 2000).

2. **Know if your listening style may feel like over or under-reacting.**

   Teresa is sharing her video clip with Yumiko. As she comments about her noticings, Yumiko is quiet. She continues to point out her thinking about her video, waiting for Yumiko to chime in or offer support to what she is saying, but she says nothing. Teresa thinks, "What is wrong with my video? There must be something wrong, which is why she doesn't know what to say." Meanwhile, Yumiko is thinking, "It's good that she is able to express what she wants, and I will wait until she has said everything she wants to say." When Teresa abruptly ends the conversation, Yumiko is puzzled.

   → Tanner (2005) talks about "high-involvement" and "high-consideration" styles in communication. Some people/cultures tend to show their engagement in the conversation by actively cutting in to agree, ask questions, and react verbally to the speaker, while others show this engagement by demonstrating their consideration for the speaker by not speaking, waiting quietly, and not interjecting. Depending on who the speaker is and the kind of listening style they expect, there can be a mismatch that leads to misunderstandings.

3. **Please, no advice!**

   Sherryl and Michael begin to watch Sherryl's video. Sherryl has told him she wants to get more participation from a particular group of students in the class. Michael stops the video and tells Sherryl he sees exactly what the issue is and proceeds to give her three to four ways she could fix the problem. Sherryl knows Michael means well and has good teaching ideas but still she dreads the rest of the session and continuing to receive all this advice. Meanwhile, Michael is getting annoyed since Sherryl does not seem to be writing all of these good tips down. He wonders what the point is if Sherryl is not going to take advantage of these suggestions.

(Continued)

(Continued)

→ Hijacking, unwelcome high involvement and unsolicited advice-giving are all related listener behaviors that may come from great intentions or simple lack of self-awareness but backfire for the speaker. Moving teachers into new conversational practices about video of practice often requires clear norms and structures in order to prevent the talk from becoming avoidant or solution oriented (Addleman, Brazo, Dixon, Cevallos, & Wortman, 2014). Refraining from offering solutions can be very difficult for educators who are expert problem solvers and who have a lot invested in the outcome of the speaker. A deterrent for advice giving comes from reactance theory, which suggests that whenever someone tells us what to do and how to do it, we respond with defiance because we want to maximize our personal freedom (Brehm & Brehm, 2013).

4. Refrain from question peppering.

Jade and Genevieve meet after school in their professional-learning hour to talk about Jade's teaching. Jade is upset about an incident that she has captured on the video and wants to express her feelings and thoughts about what occurred. Genevieve interrupts her with questions to clarify what Jade means about the class, the student, the incident, and Jade starts to wish she had never started the conversation. She tells Genevieve she needs to go to the bathroom and leaves angrier than when she began the conversation.

→ In their helpful book *Coaching Conversations*, Cheliotes and Reilly (2010) illustrate a number of ways we engage in conversations that are counterproductive. In one termed "inquisitive listening," they note that "instead of listening to the essence of the other person's message, [we] become curious about irrelevant details of the story" (p. 38). This approach can result in the speaker escalating feelings of frustration as they start to become defensive when the questions seem to suggest that they made a mistake or create doubt that the listener is really tuning into where they are. Most of the time, teachers avoid sharing reflections with others who they anticipate will barrage them with questions. Cheliotes and Reilly suggest that if we can listen to our colleagues without obligation to investigate every detail, we can become more trusted listeners.

5. Remember your body language.

Rita and Lauren are ready to discuss Lauren's video clip, and both believe they will gain much from this professional conversation. Lauren opens her laptop on the table and they review the video, which they have both previously viewed. Rita then takes her laptop out and places it on the table in front of her so she can take notes and read the notes she had already taken about Lauren's video. Lauren feels like Rita is not really listening to her since she is busily taking notes. Rita feels she is showing how seriously she takes the conversation by taking detailed notes.

→ It is said that over 80% of our communicative messages are conveyed through our body language, consisting of facial expressions, body positioning, gestures, touch, and eye contact. Even physical positioning, such as having a laptop blocking the space in front of your body or having a mobile phone sitting on the table between you and a partner, can affect how the other person experiences the listening you offer. In *What Great Listeners Actually Do* (2016), Zenger and Folkman suggest that putting away laptops and phones, making eye contact, and physically shifting toward the speaker "not only affects how you are perceived as the listener; it immediately influences the listener's *own* attitudes and inner feelings. Acting the part changes how you feel inside. This in turn makes you a better listener."

6. **Be cautious of both praise and criticism.**

Ted and Cristina are about to share their video clips. Cristina goes first, and as the video is playing, Ted is commenting about how great her classroom management is, how neat her classroom looks, and how engaged her students are in the lesson. When Cristina asks him to provide suggestions about her challenge presenting a particular math problem, he keeps emphasizing how great she is and declares he cannot come up with anything she is not already doing. Cristina feels frustrated with Ted and hopes to get a new partner next time who is more critical.

→ Sharing one's teaching on video is a highly "face-threatening" act (Brown & Levinson, 1987)—that is, it causes the conversation partner to want to lessen any tension or awkwardness experienced by the teacher who is showing their video. This leads to conversational moves like complimenting, avoiding, and agreeing in order to mitigate the confrontation. Teachers may be anticipating their own video being shared and figure if they load on the praise with their partner, they can expect the same in return. However, praise is problematic for two reasons. First, if you are praising me, that means you are evaluating me, and that means I can also be criticized, which causes anxiety. Second, if you are praising or evaluating, you are neither describing nor participating with me to see more in my teaching—you are doing that work for me. Even if you praise, I will not know exactly what components I should replicate.

7. **Be conscious of what "helping" can lead to.**

Kristen and Gina are eager to share their videos with one another. They have their clips and exchange them for viewing. Kristen is used to getting a lot of ideas from Gina, so when Gina does not seem to be helping her during their viewing session, Kristen starts to feel agitated. "Why isn't Gina telling me what she thinks?" Gina has been trying to move out of her usual role with Kristen, where she offers her a ton of support and tries to guide her. She is holding back purposefully, and she is finding it really difficult. She really wants to help Kristen and senses her agitation, so she goes back into her usual pattern of giving her opinion of the teaching on the video.

→ "Helping" out another teacher, a novice teacher, or a supervisee seems innocent and even expected. However, it can be useful to consider what our intentions are when we tell ourselves we are helping and to consider the long-term effects of helping. Fanselow (1988) points out that the one who receives help can come to resent the "helper" and reframes the observation process.

"Whereas the usual aim of observation and supervision is to help or evaluate the person being seen, the aim I propose is self-exploration—seeing one's own teaching differently. . . . Observing to explore is a process; observing to help or to evaluate is providing a product" (Fanselow, 1988, p. 115).

When teachers see themselves less as "helpers" and more as *collaborators* in exploring teaching via video, the way they will watch, listen, and ask questions will shift. Collaboration is generative and benefits all participants.

8. **Take up the believing rather than the doubting stance.**

Mark is not looking forward to sharing his video with Tim, who is supervising him this year. He is sure that the supervisor wants only to evaluate his teaching performance and find him wanting. Tim is worried that the conversation he will have with Mark will not go well. He is pretty sure Mark is resistant to all feedback and that the methods he is using to teach his class are far too traditional.

(Continued)

(Continued)

> → Elbow's (1973) concept of the *believing game* and the *doubting game* can be helpful ways of considering how we frame our conversations and our role as listeners. If we choose to view those we listen to as doing the best they can, given what they bring to the situation at that moment, we can open ourselves up as listeners and relate with more compassion (Brown, 2015). As Oprandy (1999) puts it, when we assume "a believing game stance that is focused on creating possibilities rooted in an exploratory spirit, we need not maintain a homeostatic, ritualistic kind of conversation with our counterpart" (p. 106). By listening authentically, we can create new kinds of conversations rather than engaging in the formulaic exchanges that do not motivate meaningful learning.

INTENTIONAL SPEAKING

This chapter has emphasized the importance of remembering teachers' sensitivities around video and how they may experience different listening styles when they begin to talk about their teaching via video records. Another important element to promoting productive conversations about video is to set norms for how the conversation will be conducted. Although this often feels awkward and contrived, it can actually provide the safety and clarity of expectations for both the teacher speaking about his/her video and for the educator supporting that talk. There are two essential components that can be implemented that are shown to enhance the depth of teachers' reflections.

1. ***Teachers pre-determine what is to be discussed.***

The first important element is to have the teacher whose video is being shared identify what it is *they* wish to investigate. This narrows the field of infinite possible topics and provides the teacher a sense of control over a conversation that makes them feel very vulnerable. It helps the speaker stay focused on instruction rather than reacting to themselves on video, and it helps the listener know what it is they should be attending to and discussing. When both the teacher and those listening to the teacher have clear intentions about the purpose of the viewing and the subsequent talk, it creates safety and promotes trust and creates a common aim for the viewing and discussion.

2. ***Teachers use selective questioning to promote teacher thinking.***

The second element to consider implementing when getting started with video analysis of teaching is to design questions that focus on getting the teacher the answers she is seeking to the question posed that has formed the focus of investigation. Rather than bringing in topics that the viewer finds interesting, the conversation stays focused on helping the teacher reflect on the topic that was predetermined. The questions are open ended, assume positive intent, and act as "thought-starters to energize the mind and consider new perspectives" (Cheliotes & Reilly, 2010).

Reviewing video clips, listening attentively and supportively, and asking thought-provoking questions set the stage for teachers to make powerful discoveries. Questioning that puts teachers on the defensive, however, should always be avoided. Too often, the questions we ask teachers automatically makes them feel inadequate and lead them to defensive responses rather than promoting reflection. Kimsey-House, Kimsey-House, Sandahl, and Whitworth (2011) present a wide variety of open-ended "powerful questions" that encourage a conversation partner to follow his thinking and wondering in ways that lead to discovery and action. Prompts touch on teacher's emotions, beliefs, knowledge, and experience, thus engaging the whole of the teacher in the process in order to match the intellectual and psychological aspects of seeing one's practice on video. These prompts might include the following:

- Tell me more about . . . ?

- What are you noticing about . . . ?

- What are your thoughts about . . . ?

- What does this mean to you?

- What does your intuition tell you?

- What is the opportunity here?

- What is the challenge?

- What other angles can you think of?

- If you could do it over again, what would you do differently?

- What is your desired outcome?

- Is this a time for action? What action?

Talking with all of these rules for listening and speaking can slow the process down and feel very strange at first. Using a tool such as a script like the one below can be helpful to introduce and practice these new conversational norms.

Sample Protocol for Participants Sharing Video in Pairs

Teacher A. (The teacher sharing the video)

Before showing your video to your partner, complete the following:

1. My video clip is of my _____ class. It's about _____ minutes long and takes place at the _____ of the lesson.

2. When I watched my video, I noticed _____, _____, and _____.

3. I am hoping you can carefully observe _____ with me today.

4. I would like to be asked to think more about _____ today.

(Continued)

(Continued)

Teacher B. (The teacher watching and supporting the video-recorded teacher)

Before discussing the video clip you just watched, complete the following:

1. My partner's video clip is of his/her _____ class.

2. When I watch his/her video, I will carefully observe _____.

3. I will ask him/her to think more about _____ today. I will phrase my questions like this: _____.

When facilitating a professional-learning session that is introducing video, the facilitator can take on the part of Teacher A and provide endings to those sentence starters and then share his or her own video. After stopping the video, participants can take on the role of Teacher B and work on the phrasing of their questions, which can then be reviewed as a group. Usually there a number of questions that will cause defensiveness. These can be reworked together. Then, a volunteer can take on Teacher B's role in having a conversation and the considerations for intentional listening can be rehearsed. This could all take place before the partnered teachers ever actually look at their own videos together.

PUTTING IDEAS INTO ACTION

Let's return to the case presented at the start of this chapter where video was introduced to support a new teacher's learning, but it did not start off going well. We can now see that there are several steps that were skipped over that led to this all-too-common, result. Despite the coach and teacher's best intentions, what was missing in this approach? In what ways does this vignette relate to your own practice?

1. What could Marcus have done to ensure that the conversation would have been more comfortable and productive for Lizzy?

2. What principles of listening might have improved the conversation?

3. What could Marcus do now so that the next time they talk about video it is a more positive experience?

4. What has your experience been with having conversations about teaching with colleagues?

5. Which parts of this chapter resonate for you in terms of facilitating other teachers' conversations or for your own use of video analysis?

Chapter References

Addleman, R. A., Brazo, C. J., Dixon, K., Cevallos, T., & Wortman, S. (2014). Teacher candidates' perceptions of debriefing circles to facilitate self-reflection during a cultural immersion experience. *The New Educator, 10*(2), 112–128.

Brehm, S. S., & Brehm, J. W. (2013). *Psychological reactance: A theory of freedom and control.* Cambridge, MA: Academic Press.

Brown, B. (2015). *Rising strong.* New York, NY: Random House.

Brown, P., & Levinson, S. C. (1987). *Politeness: Some universals in language usage* (Vol. 4). New York, NY: Cambridge University Press.

Cheliotes, L. M. G., & Reilly, M. F. (2010). *Coaching conversations: Transforming your school one conversation at a time*. Thousand Oaks, CA: Corwin Press.

Elbow, P. (1973). The doubting game and the believing game, Appendix. *Writing without teachers*. New York, NY: Oxford University Press.

Fanselow, J. F. (1988). "Let's see": Contrasting conversations about teaching. *TESOL Quarterly*, *22*(1), 113–130.

Fuller, F. F., & Manning, B. A. (1973). Self-confrontation reviewed: A conceptualization for video playback in teacher education. *Review of Educational Research*, *43*(4), 469–528.

Kimsey-House, H., Kimsey-House, K., Sandahl, P., & Whitworth, L. (2011). *Co-active coaching: Changing business, transforming lives* (3rd ed.). London, United Kingdom: Nicholas Brealey.

Kochan, F. K., & Trimble, S. B. (2000). From mentoring to co-mentoring: Establishing collaborative relationships. *Theory into Practice*, *39*(1), 20–28.

Oprandy, R. (1999). Exploring with a supervisor. In J. G. Gebhard & R. Oprandy (Eds.). *Language teaching awareness: A guide to exploring beliefs and practices* (pp. 99–121). Cambridge, MA: Cambridge University Press.

Ronchi, D., & Ripple, R. E. (1972). *Videotaped playback: To see ourselves as others see us*. Chicago, IL: American Educational Research Association.

Tanner, D. (2005). *Conversational style: Analyzing talk among friends*. New York, NY: Oxford University Press.

Ueland, B. (1993). Tell me more: On the fine art of listening. In B. Ueland, *Strength to your sword arm: Selected writings*. Duluth, MN: Holy Cow! Press. Retrieved from http://physics.uwyo.edu/~ddale/research/REU/2016/Tell_Me_More.pdf

Zenger, J., & Folkman, J. (2016). What great listeners actually do. *Harvard Business Review*. Retrieved from https://hbr.org/2016/07/what-great-listeners-actually-do

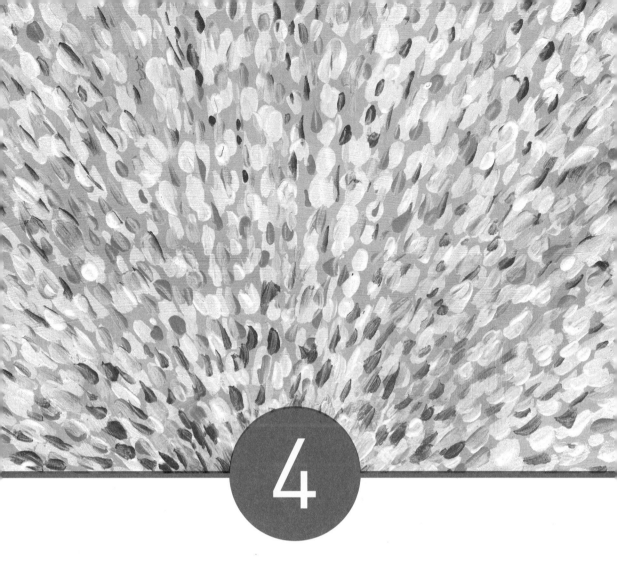

4

WHAT ARE THE TECHNICAL ASPECTS OF CREATING VIDEO RECORDINGS OF TEACHING?

Technology is the campfire around which we tell our stories.

—Laurie Anderson

CHAPTER OBJECTIVES

- To review best practices in capturing, editing, storing, and sharing video of teaching

- To share sample consent and permission forms that respect and protect teachers and students

Once the decision to utilize video in teacher learning has been made, technology requirements are usually the next aspect of implementation that facilitators consider. Simply put—how will the video material get produced? Concerns usually arise when teachers hear they are to video record themselves, and facilitators may wonder how they will obtain video materials that will fit with the teacher-learning tasks they are designing. When starting out, it is usually easier to search for videos of teaching that can be found via the Internet rather than asking teachers to video record themselves. Chapter 10 provides a list of such resources as well as a process for curating available video. Indeed, much high-quality video can be obtained online. However, there are important limitations when resourcing video from open-access sites. For instance, videos of teaching found online may lack authenticity if they

- Feature staged, "phony" episodes

- Are heavily edited with teacher interviews, leaving limited raw classroom footage

- Show classroom settings very remote from the experiences of participating teachers

- Lack the instructional focus desired for the particular professional development being planned

Thus, creating one's own video is essential in order to have footage uniquely suited to a particular professional-learning focus and for teachers to get to see themselves, the ultimate goal of video analysis. This chapter suggests guidelines for the technical aspects of video capture, editing, storage, and sharing as well as the ethical elements of consent, privacy, buy-in, and safety when supporting teachers video recording themselves to create video materials for analysis.

CAPTURING VIDEO FOR TEACHER-LEARNING PURPOSES

When teachers participate in video clubs or other professional-learning formats to examine their practice, it is recommended that facilitators do not ask teachers to video record themselves right away, as this is something that is best approached slowly and once trust in the process has been established (Baecher, Rorimer, & Smith, 2012). Instead, facilitators can begin by asking participants to examine video of an "unknown other" classroom—video taken from a similar class but not from anyone they know. This is done to reduce anxiety and so teachers can learn the skills of video analysis before trying it out on their own and their peers' video.

Once teachers do start to capture and share video from their own classrooms, facilitators will want to provide some clear guidelines and suggestions to reduce the technical barriers as much as possible. After the privacy, permission, and consent process has been clarified (see section on this later in this chapter), teachers should be provided with information about how to set up, capture, edit, and share videos from their classrooms. When this information is provided, the video quality is much higher and the resulting video footage more useful for the facilitator to potentially archive for future use.

The following guidelines for recording and analyzing video of teaching are adapted from the instructions on video analysis provided in the handbook for the National Board for Professional Teaching Standards (2015). These are presented in five areas: (1) technology assistance; (2) video recording equipment; (3) audio quality; (4) camera positioning; and (5) desensitization.

TECHNOLOGY ASSISTANCE

While some teachers will not need assistance in the video-recording process, it can still be helpful to find colleagues or others who have the expertise or availability to assist and allow the focus to be on the teaching and not on the technology. Possibilities include the following:

- Checking with a district or school-based technology educator, library media, or audiovisual specialist

- Inquiring at colleges of education for fieldwork students who could assist with video recording

- Seeing whether colleagues or high school students may be able to help out with video recording and video editing

- Overviewing the process can help relieve teachers' anxiety—for example, as done in this video, which is under five minutes: https://www
.teachingchannel.org/video/videotaping-tips-for-teachers

VIDEO-RECORDING EQUIPMENT

Perhaps contrary to belief, access to high quality or professional-grade video-recording equipment is neither necessary nor recommended for teachers to video capture their teaching for professional-learning purposes. When teachers have to use equipment that is complicated and unfamiliar, they are much more anxious, more likely to focus on the obstacles to video than the benefits, and to have their attention drawn to the camera's presence rather than their teaching. Therefore, encouraging teachers to use their own digital recording devices—cell phones, laptops, tablets—is highly preferable. This video in general is used for a specific learning purpose and then discarded, so it does not have to be Hollywood quality.

When teachers record with their own devices, they are more comfortable, know how to charge the device and troubleshoot, and understand how and where the video is stored after filming. Schools and other institutions can also provide loaner devices, such as tablets or video cameras with small tripods.

If a cell phone, tablet, or digital video camera is used, a tripod is an essential additional tool to reduce shakiness; the camera should never be held by a person but rather be lifted and repositioned as necessary. An extension cord can be helpful as well so that the concern of batteries running out mid-recording can be eliminated. Test runs are recommended for teachers to figure out, for the device they are using, how long the battery will last and how long the camera will record before shutting off or reaching memory capacity. Spending some time playing with video recording on the device—even outside the classroom—goes a long way to ensuring comfort and knowledge when it is time to capture classroom video.

AUDIO QUALITY

Audio quality is important and can be the most troublesome aspect of classroom-video recording. Hearing the teacher is usually easier than hearing student talk. The busy classroom environment, coupled with poor room acoustics, make capturing classroom audio a challenge. A few strategies can help improve audio quality:

- Before each recording session, it can be helpful to check the equipment to be sure that all cables are secured, as faulty connections can cause unwanted background noise.

- Other background noise can also diminish sound quality, so teachers can look to see if fans, air conditioners, and outside noise like recess or band practice can be minimized. Using a tripod or propping the recording device and not touching it unnecessarily are important to reduce noise from movement.

- The built-in microphone of most cameras is generally not adequate. Because it is attached to the camera, it is frequently not close enough to the person speaking, so it often picks up background noise and misses important conversations. Using an external microphone is the most effective way to enhance sound quality. There are inexpensive ones that can be connected to cell phones, tablets, and laptop computers.

- Keeping the microphone close to the action is the most important aspect of capturing high-quality audio. If the teacher will be circulating among student groups, for example, consider carrying an external microphone. For whole-class recording, the external microphone can be placed in the center of the room.

POSITIONING THE CAMERA

Using a tripod, the video camera should be positioned and repositioned to best align with the observation goals of the video analysis. It is helpful for teachers to think through where they and their students will be in the space of the classroom during the activities to be portrayed on the videotape and consider a variety of questions:

- How will the room be set up?
- Where will the teacher be/move during the lesson?
- Where will the students be?
- Where will the camera be?
- What will the camera "see"?
- Will the camera stay in one place or be moved as the lesson progresses to show things from a different perspective?
- How long with the lesson be?
- When will the recording be started/stopped?
- Will different activities require students to regroup and move around the classroom?
- How will the use of instructional materials be recorded?
- What must the camera absolutely need to capture?

Meeting with the camera operator, if it is not the teacher, to plan prior to video recording, along with sharing the lesson plan, can aid in the discussion of plans to best capture the teaching and learning. The following suggestions are also generally recommended:

- If using a phone or tablet, make sure to hold the camera to capture horizontally, not vertically.
- Avoid any panning or zooming—instead, move the camera closer to the action or reposition it.
- If chalkboard and/or whiteboard writing is an important part of the lesson, be sure that it is captured on the video recording and is legible. This may require refocusing the lens on the board. In addition, sometimes writing is legible to the eye but not to the camera, so you might have to move the camera to reduce the amount of glare on the board.
- Increase the amount of light in the classroom to improve the video recording. Be sure to turn on all the lights and, if possible, open curtains or blinds.
- Never shoot directly into bright light. If there are windows on one side of the classroom or a smartboard, try to shoot with your back to that light source.
- For capturing whole-class interaction, it may be optimal to place the camera up high and to the side of the room to capture the students and teacher. It is not recommended to try to follow a conversation back and forth between different people; the camera always arrives late to the action.

View of whole classroom showing best camera placement

- For capturing small groups, plan ahead to determine the group of students to be video recorded and then place the camera on a tripod, choosing a single vantage point. It is important for viewers to be able to see and hear the group interaction.

View of a small group showing best camera and microphone placement

DESENSITIZATION

When a video camera enters a classroom, both teachers and students can become anxious and react to its presence. This can result in students being afraid to speak or the opposite, hamming it up in front of the camera. Teachers may feel nervous about the technology working or just feel self-conscious, with the video-recording process vying for their attention. Some teachers can ignore the presence of the camera if someone else is in the room to manage it, while for other teachers, someone else managing the camera creates the same stress as an observation visit. In this case, it is advisable for the teacher to work with a device and process that enables them to video record easily on their own.

In general, the more that teachers control their own video-recording process—using their own equipment, setting up and recording without assistance—the more likely they are to video record on a regular basis. Over a few trials, this desensitizes both the teacher and the students to the presence of the camera and results in authentic footage. There are even bases, such as *Swivl* (https://www.swivl .com/), to place a video-recording device that rotates, tracking the teacher's movements around the room. However, if the device creates complications or confusion, it is best to use the easiest, simplest approach, as the video is not intended to be a professional production but a data collection tool.

Another recommendation is to begin with video recording only 10 minutes or so of the lesson—for instance, video recording class openings, closures, or small group work. Then, the camera can be shut off. This reduces stress, focuses the nature of the resulting clips, creates smaller files that are easier to manage and edit, and acclimates teachers to the whole video-recording process. Watching a few of these short clips without the intention to share them can help teachers understand how to better place the camera, the kinds of interactions that can be observed with video, and can incentivize further video recording (Baecher, Kung, Jewkes, & Rosalia, 2013).

VIDEO EDITING, COMPRESSION, AND SHARING

Once the video has been captured, learning how to move it to a computer and to store or share it is the next step, so that the video file can be deleted from the recording device. When the video file is first downloaded from a camcorder or a portable digital device, it is generally (if of a lesson of 30–50 minutes) too large a file to directly email or upload. This is because video is usually recorded in "high definition." The following image helps to show how the measurement of the pixels in the video create a larger or smaller file size. HD videos are measured at 1,920 × 1,080 pixels. The objective is to save the file so that it is closer to "standard definition"—1,280 × 720 pixels or 640 × 360 pixels. Standard definition is typically a size that works for uploading to online platforms.

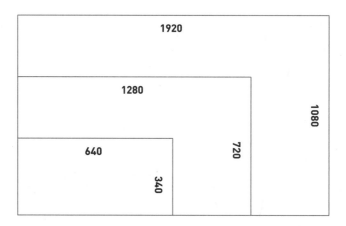

The other two features to consider are the length of the video in overall minutes and the video's bits per second (bps). An HD video that runs for one minute will become a 100 MB file—really huge when those minutes add up. On the other hand, if that same video were compressed down to a standard definition of 640 × 360, then one minute would be 10 MB. This is why compressing video files is going to make upload and sharing much easier. Free tools are available to compress video, such as *Windows Live Movie Maker* and *iMovie.*

When video recordings are being made for assessment purposes, editing is usually prohibited. This is the case for teachers entering the profession (edTPA (https://www.edtpa.com/), experienced teachers seeking national certification (NBPTS (https://www.nbpts.org/), or even where video recorded lessons are used for teacher evaluation purposes. In teacher-learning contexts, however, editing is common. For example, one 40-minute lesson could be edited multiple ways, resulting in many 2- to 10-minute clips, depending upon the goals of the video analysis tasks. Shorter clips are much more conducive for analysis than long ones. There are many tools for editing that make the process fairly straightforward—for example: *iMovie, Quicktime Pro, Windows Movie Maker* and others. The output of smaller clips should be of a file size that is easy to share, depending upon the sharing platform, but usually ranging from 25MB to 200MB. When teachers are going to share portions of their lessons, they often do not need to actually edit the video but simply note the start and stop time on their video of the sections they are ready to share. Time stamping is a lot easier than physically editing or excerpting and often works well for most activities.

In general, it is empowering for teachers to "own" their video and make their own determinations about which clips they are willing to share. This means that showing teachers how to save and edit the video they have captured is necessary. Considerations of privacy—of utmost importance once video clips are created and ready to be shared—are addressed in the following section.

CONSIDERATIONS OF PRIVACY, CONFIDENTIALITY, AND CONSENT

Video recording in classrooms requires thoughtful attention to issues surrounding protection of students' and teachers' privacy. Because the video constitutes a shareable, possibly public artifact, it is quite different from observing classrooms live and therefore necessitates a series of steps to ensure that all those who appear in the video understand their rights and how the video will be used. The three phases outlined below can serve as a guide.

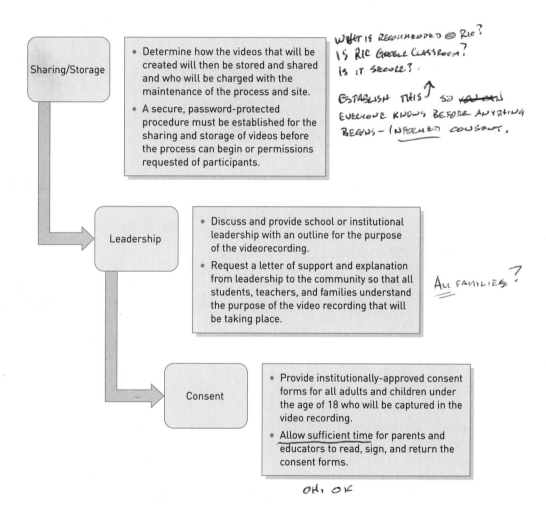

Sharing/Storage
- Determine how the videos that will be created will then be stored and shared and who will be charged with the maintenance of the process and site.
- A secure, password-protected procedure must be established for the sharing and storage of videos before the process can begin or permissions requested of participants.

[handwritten: WHAT IS RECOMMENDED @ RIC? IS RIC GOOGLE CLASSROOM? IS IT SECURE? ESTABLISH THIS ↑ SO everyone EVERYONE KNOWS BEFORE ANYTHING BEGINS — INFORMED CONSENT.]

Leadership
- Discuss and provide school or institutional leadership with an outline for the purpose of the videorecording.
- Request a letter of support and explanation from leadership to the community so that all students, teachers, and families understand the purpose of the video recording that will be taking place.

[handwritten: ALL FAMILIES?]

Consent
- Provide institutionally-approved consent forms for all adults and children under the age of 18 who will be captured in the video recording.
- Allow sufficient time for parents and educators to read, sign, and return the consent forms.

[handwritten: OH, OK]

SHARING AND STORAGE

First, staffing must be considered in regards to the development, maintenance, and support within a school, district, or college. Who will have the authority, discretion, and responsibility for ensuring that the procedures of privacy and consent are consistently upheld? Who will provide technical guidance and troubleshoot video capturing, editing, and sharing? And who will oversee the process to reduce additional stress and anxiety for participant teachers? Depending on the scale of the project, a working group or a particular coach or faculty member can make these determinations.

It is recommended that the procedures for where video will be stored and how steps will be taken to ensure participants' privacy are clearly outlined as part of the consent/permission form process. Suggested procedural outlines for video storage and sharing are provided below: These procedures could be adapted for the specific platform or online sharing/storage used in the particular setting. These might include a cloud service such as *Google Drive for Education* (https://edu.google.com/) or *Dropbox* (www.dropbox.com/); portfolio systems such as *Chalk & Wire* (www.chalkandwire.com/) or *Taskstream* (https://www.taskstream.com/); or video-focused platforms such as *Vimeo* (https://vimeo.com/) and *Vialogues* (https://vialogues.com/). It is strongly recommended that an institution select one or two approved platforms rather than allow members of the community to pick different ones. When too many systems are used, the risk of breaches to privacy are greater and the burden on the staff who maintain the process increases.

Any system selected should be password protected and FERPA compliant. FERPA (https://www2.ed.gov/policy/gen/guid/fpco/ferpa/index.html) is a federal law that protects the privacy of students' educational records—it is thus applicable to both K–12 learners as well as teacher education students in colleges and graduate schools. FERPA compliance means ensuring that the videos of K–12 students as well as teacher candidates, when used via mobile applications (apps) or web-based tools, have protective firewalls in place to avoid any data breaches.

LEADERSHIP SUPPORT

Very often educators are concerned about introducing video analysis into professional development work, and a strong sign of support from institutional leadership is absolutely essential. When leaders, such as principals, superintendents, or deans at colleges of teacher education communicate their enthusiasm and support for video analysis of teaching, the barriers are readily overcome and teachers, parents, and professors can feel not only more comfortable with the work but recognized for it.

INFORMED CONSENT

Every K–12 school, college of teacher education, or other educational institution engaged in video recording and analysis of classroom video will need to ensure that the informed consent process is followed. Informed consent must be obtained by parents/guardians for pupils to appear in videos but also from student teachers, cooperating teachers, and other adults in the videos. The American Association of

Colleges for Teacher Education (AACTE, n.d.) outlines five important principles that should be present when engaging in classroom video recording:

1. The purpose of classroom videos should be to support teacher and student learning.

2. Parents/guardians should be asked to sign permission forms before video recording commences.

3. Anyone whose job involves access to classroom videos "should have clear rules and guidelines for how to collect, use, protect, and destroy the videos."

4. Classroom videos should never be used for informational or marketing purposes without parent/guardian permission.

5. "Any educational institution that collects or stores classroom video should have a policy for notifying families of any misuse" and include a contact name for questions.

This process should be guided by legal advice and approval by ethics review as relevant to each context.

SAMPLE LETTERS AND STATEMENTS

These letters may be helpful in getting the process started and can be adapted for use in local settings. They should always be reviewed by legal and administrative advisors before being adopted. Below are samples which may be relevant in both the K–12 and higher education contexts.

Sample Policy Statement on Video Storage and Sharing

Context: K–12 schools or institutions of teacher education

Purpose: Use of video recording and analysis for teacher learning

Who For: Teachers and teacher candidates participating in video recording, colleagues who will view/access video

[Letterhead/Logo of Educational Institution]

Policies for Video Storage and Sharing

At [SCHOOL/INSTITUTION NAME], we believe strongly in the importance of video analysis of teaching as a core practice in advancing teacher learning. We also understand the sensitivities and caution that must be taken around the video artifacts to protect the privacy of teachers and students. Therefore, we require that every member of our learning community adhere to the following:

1. [SCHOOL/INSTITUTION NAME]-issued parent/guardian permission forms and teacher consent forms must be secured before any video recording is conducted. No other permission/consent forms may substitute. Permission/consent forms should be saved in a secure location for three years from the date of signing.

2. All video records must be uploaded to [FERPA APPROVED PLATFORM], and the original video record must be deleted and trashed from local cameras, digital devices, and laptops once the video record has been uploaded.

3. Video records should not have any last names of teachers, students, or school-identifying information in the file name or within the video itself.

4. Video records may be accessed for review by other members of the [SCHOOL/INSTITUTION NAME] community only by logging into [FERPA APPROVED PLATFORM] using [SCHOOL/INSTITUTION NAME]-issued, [FERPA]-approved log in credentials. This log in may not be shared at any time.

5. Video records are never to be downloaded from [FERPA APPROVED PLATFORM], stored on personal drives or other platforms, distributed, or shared outside of [FERPA APPROVED PLATFORM] within our [SCHOOL/INSTITUTION NAME] community.

If any member of the [SCHOOL/INSTITUTION NAME] community fails to abide by these policies, [SCHOOL/INSTITUTION NAME] will take action against me that in its sole discretion [SCHOOL/INSTITUTION NAME] deems appropriate. Such action may include but is not limited to the following: failing a class; revoking earned credits, degrees or licenses; suspension or expulsion; reporting of the infraction to law enforcement, licensing authorities, or current or future employers.

These policies are in place to protect K–12 pupils, teacher candidates, and teachers as they embark with trust and security in this powerful teacher development opportunity. Knowing that the video records they create will only be used for teacher-learning purposes within our community is essential to the process. Thank you for your attention and for respecting these polices. Please contact [NAME, PHONE, EMAIL] with any questions or concerns or to report any violation of these policies.

Sample Letter From College of Education Dean

Context: Teacher education

Purpose: Use of video recording and analysis for teacher certification

Who Reads: K–12 school leaders, cooperating teachers, district leaders

[Letterhead/Logo of Educational Institution]

To: Principal, Partner School

From: [NAME], Dean, [INSTITUTION NAME]

Subject: Video recording of teacher candidates

One of the requirements of the teacher preparation programs at [INSTITUTION NAME] is the videotaping of lessons for the purpose of learning about and improving teaching practice. Each of our teacher candidates at [INSTITUTION NAME] is required to video record lessons from the classroom and later to analyze and discuss the video with supervising faculty. This allows a unique opportunity to observe key interactions between student and teacher that are critical for effective instruction. Thus, in addition to the on-site observations by [INSTITUTION NAME] supervisors, student teachers at your school will video record several classes.

In accordance with the policies of the [SCHOOL DISTRICT NAME], we need to ensure that the parents/guardians of students who might appear in the videotape have given their consent. In some schools, this consent has already been arranged and need not be granted again. If you need to get consent from the students in question, student teachers will work with host teachers to ensure that every student in the video recording has submitted a signed permission form. Completed consent forms will be collected by teacher candidates and returned to [INSTITUTION NAME] for our records.

In addition, we ask that cooperating/mentor/host teachers also sign their consent to appear in the video recordings. The video material will be used only by the teacher candidate and by selected [INSTITUTION NAME] faculty for the purposes of instruction and research; no video will ever be released to the public. (*WITHOUT PERMISSION*) *PURPOSE OF MODEL VIDEO LIBRARY IS PUBLIC...*

If you have any questions about the videotaping, please feel free to contact [NAME at INSTITUTION] at [PHONE NUMBER] or [EMAIL].

I appreciate your willingness to work with our teacher candidates and look forward to your continued collaboration with [INSTITUTION NAME].

Sample Letter From School District Leader

Context: K–12 school district

Purpose: Use of video recording and analysis for teacher development

Who Reads: Parents of K–12 pupils, teachers, coaches, building leaders

[Letterhead/Logo of Educational Institution]

To: Parents, Teachers, District Staff

From: [NAME], [SCHOOL DISTRICT NAME]

Subject: Video recording of teaching

One of the most powerful ways to improve the quality of teaching is to engage teachers in reflection on their practice via the analysis of video records of lessons. At [SCHOOL DISTRICT NAME], we are engaging in professional development initiatives that will invite teachers to video record lessons from the classroom and later to analyze and discuss the video with colleagues, school leaders, and supervisors. This will allow for unique opportunities to observe key interactions between student and teacher that are critical for effective instruction.

In accordance with the policies of the [SCHOOL DISTRICT NAME], we need to ensure that the parents/guardians of students who might appear in the videotape have given their consent. In some schools, this consent has already been arranged and need not be granted again. If you need to get consent from the students in question, teachers will work to ensure that every student in the video recording has submitted a signed permission form. Completed consent forms will be collected and stored by teachers.

The video material will be used only by the teachers in our district for the purposes of instruction and program improvement; no video will ever be released to the public.

If you have any questions about the videotaping, please feel free to contact [NAME at SCHOOL DISTRICT] at [PHONE NUMBER] or [EMAIL].

Sample Parent/Guardian Consent Letter

Context: K–12 school

Purpose: Use of video recording and analysis for teacher development

Who Signs: Parents of K–12 pupils

[Letterhead/Logo of Educational Institution]

Video/Artifact Consent

Parent/Guardian Consent

Dear Parent/Guardian (or pupil at least 18 years old):

Your child may have a teacher in their classroom who is participating in ongoing professional learning to improve their teaching effectiveness. As part of this process, teachers at [SCHOOL NAME] are sharing lessons they planned, video/audio recordings of a classroom lesson, and samples of student work they have graded. Some of these materials may also be used to train other student teachers, faculty, and staff. These materials will be viewed under secure, password-protected conditions, never posted on publicly accessible websites. While the teachers are instructed not to mention pupils by name in their video/audio submissions, pupils may appear in the video or their voices may be heard at certain times during the recording. Additionally, the samples of graded work submitted as part of the teacher candidate's portfolio will not include any pupils' names or other identifying information.

Please complete the form below to indicate whether or not you grant permission for your child's participation in these activities. Thank you for your consideration and for your support. Please do not hesitate to contact [Name/email/phone] with any questions or concerns.

PERMISSION FORM

Pupil Name: _____   Classroom Teacher: _____

School: _____   Semester/Year: _____

I am the parent/legal guardian of the child named above. I have received and read your letter regarding video recording in my child's classroom and agree to the following: (Please initial the appropriate blank below.)

_____I DO give permission for my child to appear on a video recording and for work samples to be saved and understand my child's name will not appear in any material written accompanying the recording.

_____I DO NOT give permission for my child to appear on the video recording and understand that he/she will still participate in any lesson but not be within view of the video camera during those times.

I have read this document prior to signing it, and I understand its contents.

Signature of Parent/Legal Guardian: _____

Printed Name: _____

Date: _____

Sample Teacher Consent Letter

Context: K–12 district teacher professional development

Purpose: Use of video recording and analysis for teacher development

Who Signs: Participant teachers

[Letterhead/Logo of Educational Institution]

Recording of Teaching

Teacher Agreement, Acknowledgement, and Release

Teacher Name: Semester/Year:

Teaching Site(s):

I, _____(teacher's name)_____, am participating in ongoing professional development to improve my teaching effectiveness. As part of this process, I am sharing lesson plans, video/audio recordings of my lessons, and samples of student work I have graded with colleagues in a professional-learning community. Some of these materials may also be used to train other student teachers, faculty, and staff. I acknowledge that when I video record my teaching in classrooms, I will follow all university and host school policies related to my activities. My video recordings may involve pupils, including pupils who are minors, and I agree that I will obtain all necessary permission from the pupils, pupils' parents/guardians (including signed "Permission to Videotape)."

I further understand and agree that any video recordings I make are intended and shall be used for the limited purposes of improving my teaching. I understand that I may be asked to share my video with peers and that all video recordings of teaching I make will only be stored or shared in the designated platform provided by the [SCHOOL DISTRICT NAME]. I agree that I will not use the recordings for any other purposes.

I have read this document prior to signing it and I understand its contents.

Signature:

Printed Name:

Date: _____

Sample Student Teacher Consent Letter

Context: College of teacher education

Purpose: Use of video recording and analysis for student teaching or fieldwork

Who Signs: Student teachers/teacher candidates in a teacher education program

[Letterhead/Logo of Educational Institution]

Recording of Supervised Teaching/Fieldwork

Teacher Candidate Agreement, Acknowledgement, and Release

Teacher Candidate Name: Semester/Year:

Teaching Site(s):

I, _____(teacher candidate's name)_____, acknowledge that when I video record my teaching in classrooms in conjunction with my coursework at the [INSTITUTION NAME College of Education], I will follow all university and host school policies related to my activities. I understand that the video recording may be on my personal electronic device, if permitted, and that such video recording is required for my course work. My video recordings may involve pupils, including pupils who are minors, and I agree that I will obtain all necessary permission from the pupils, pupils' parents/guardians (including signed "Permission to Videotape" form provided by [INSTITUTION NAME College of Education]), and relevant school/district officials to perform such recordings.

I further understand and agree that any video recordings I make are intended and shall be used for the limited purposes of improving my teaching or applying for a teaching license or teaching position where the application requires an exemplar recording of my student-experience. I understand that I may be asked to share my video with peers and in future teacher education courses and that all video recordings of teaching I make will only be stored or shared in the designated platform provided by the [INSTITUTION NAME College of Education]. I agree that I will not use the recordings for any other purposes.

I assume all liability for and agree to indemnify, defend, and hold harmless [INSTITUTION NAME College of Education], its trustees, directors, agents, and employees for any and all claims, suits, losses, costs, and expenses arising from my creation, use, misuse or distribution of the recordings. I acknowledge and agree that if I fail to abide by this agreement, [INSTITUTION NAME College of Education] will take action against me that in its sole discretion [INSTITUTION NAME College of Education] deems appropriate. Such action may include but is not limited to the following: failing the class; revoking my earned credits, degrees or licenses; suspension or expulsion; reporting me to law enforcement, licensing authorities, or current or future employers.

I have read this document prior to signing it and I understand its contents.

Signature:

Printed Name:

Date: _____

IDEAS INTO ACTION

In reviewing the technical considerations for video analysis of teaching, what do you now see as valuable—even essential—before beginning the process?

1. What experiences have you had with video recording, editing, or compression of video files?

2. What are your concerns about bringing video-recording devices into the classroom?

3. How do you envision your school community—parents, administrators, staff—reacting to the idea of video recording in the classrooms? What do you think would be important to ensure their support?

4. What device might you use for recording? Which platforms for video sharing and storage make the most sense in your context?

5. Which parts of this chapter do you think would be useful to share with teachers in terms of getting the video-recording process started in your context?

Chapter References

American Association of Colleges for Teacher Education. (n.d.). *Privacy and classroom video recordings for teacher preparation*. Retrieved from https://secure.aacte.org/apps/rl/res_get .php?fid=2530&ref=res

Baecher, L., Kung, S. C., Jewkes, A., & Rosalia, C. (2013). The role of video for self-evaluation in early field experiences. *Teaching and Teacher Education, 36*, 189–197.

Baecher, L., Rorimer, S., & Smith, L. (2012). Video-mediated teacher collaborative inquiry: Focus on English language learners. *The High School Journal, 95*(3), 49–61.

National Board for Professional Teaching Standards. (2015). *General portfolio instructions*. Retrieved from https://www.nbpts.org/wp-content/uploads/General_Portfolio_Instructions .pdf

20 VIDEO ANALYSIS TASKS

A Guide for Practice

One of the challenges facing prospective facilitators when implementing video analysis is the lack of specific protocols to follow. In this part of the text, twenty video analysis tasks that are either original or unique adaptations of existing protocols are presented in detail. Each focuses on a particular aspect of teaching to illustrate the video analysis task. Templates that facilitators can use to guide participants in a step-wise manner are included for further clarity.

Moving in sequence from Chapter 5 to subsequent chapters is strongly recommended, as Chapter 5 presents "learning to look" tasks that should always be implemented prior to advancing to more open-ended viewing activities. Chapter 6 continues with scaffolded viewing tasks that engage practitioners with data from video in ways that can promote deeper insights into the richness of video as a material for understanding classroom interaction. Chapter 7 continues to build a learning community through video analysis approaches that reinforce the connections between lesson planning and lesson delivery. Chapters 8 and 9 are designed for the coach or supervisor who will be working one-on-one with teachers whether in a developmental or an evaluative approach. Finally, Chapter 10 offers facilitators suggestions for developing a personalized collection of videos for use in professional learning.

Taken together, these practice-based tasks are designed based on thoughtful consideration of the research, which is highlighted within each section. It is also essential that facilitators review Part 1 of this text to ensure that the tasks in Part 2 are introduced after the foundations of nonjudgmental observation, expectations for interaction, and technical considerations have been reviewed. Teachers should experience these video analysis activities in a supportive, positive manner and in the spirit of learning and growth.

PART TWO

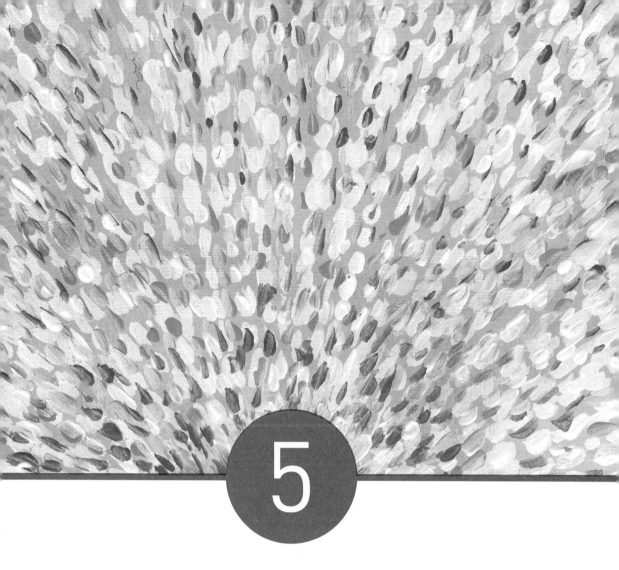

5

VIDEO USED TO INTRODUCE CLASSROOM OBSERVATION

To see a world in a grain of sand

And a heaven in a wild flower

Hold infinity in the palm of your hand

And eternity in an hour

—William Blake

CHAPTER OBJECTIVES

- To provide a perspective for looking at classroom interaction drawn from microethnography

- To underscore the need for introductory video analysis tasks that support teacher noticing

- To suggest techniques that can be varied for use in introducing teachers to video analysis of classroom practice

As seen in Part 1, there are a number of important steps to take before introducing teachers to video analysis activities. When these are skipped over, the benefits not only decrease for teacher learning, but teachers can actively refuse to participate and perceive the process negatively. However, when teachers' vulnerabilities are considered, the technological and logistical procedures are simplified, ways of looking nonjudgmentally are practiced, and norms of communication are established—teachers are excited about getting started. This chapter provides a detailed description of four approaches that are easily adapted to specific pedagogical foci and can introduce teachers to video analysis that is low stakes and low risk. These approaches, as the William Blake quote suggests, take advantage of the possibilities inherent in reviewing video, to pause and carefully look, and to see patterns emerge that reveal the universe of interactional behaviors seen across classrooms. Using highly structured tasks, such as the ones suggested in this chapter, can increase teachers' comfort level with video analysis, deepen their appreciation for the complexity of classroom observation, and lay a foundation for more open-ended and less-structured video-based reflections on teaching further down the road.

MICROETHNOGRAPHY AS AN APPROACH FOR EXPLORING TEACHING

In Chapter 1, increasing teachers' noticing skills and developing professional vision is discussed as a primary outcome of video analysis activities. But *how* do those noticing skills develop? Thinking of observing classrooms as a form of research gets at the essence of this professional learning: collecting data as objectively as possible, examining that data with an eye to a particular focus, and using findings for future inquiry. These are the components of research methods and part of video analysis of teaching. Within research methods, the tools of microethnography are particularly relevant to the initial development of teacher noticing.

Microethnography is influenced by and interrelated with ethnomethodology (the study of human behavior) and conversation analysis (the study of how talk negotiates and reflects relationships), utilizing a variety of observation methods well suited for video analysis. Microethnography seeks to explain events at the social and interactional level via the microcosm of each human interaction (Hellermann & Jakonen, 2015). Like seeing "a world in a grain of sand," microethnography typically involves meticulous attention to classroom lessons and the moment-to-moment interactions between students and teachers in order to better understand how teachers and learners interact and thus arrive at particular outcomes (Hornberger, 1995). Microethnographic approaches involve studying "how human realities are produced, activities are conducted, and sense is made, by inspecting video recordings of actual events frame by frame" (Streeck & Mehus, 2005, p. 382).

Video analysis is intrinsically tied to microethnographic methods, as these require focusing on small moments of classroom interaction, using transcription, counting, mapping, and describing rather than judging or evaluating larger swaths of teaching. Yet because we are accustomed to making evaluations quickly and coming to conclusions when we observe, microethnographic approaches can feel slowed down, awkward, or tedious. Many times teachers will exclaim, "But we only analyzed five minutes of video! How can we really know how the lesson went?" Or, "How can we know if the teaching was 'good'"? Indeed, microethnographic methods are designed to closely examine small segments of lessons and cannot and should not be used for evaluation. This kind of close looking is about exploring teach*ing* and not the teach*er*.

INTRODUCING TEACHERS TO VIDEO ANALYSIS OF TEACHING

As discussed in Part 1, working on low-inference, nonjudgmental observation of teaching is an essential precursor to effective video analysis activities. While those activities can be practiced on live observations, they are much easier to facilitate when doing so with a video of teaching. Whether teachers are preservice, in-service, or even those with supervision training and experience, tasks that utilize microethnography can significantly advance teachers' noticing skills.

While there are many types of video analysis of teaching (VAT) activities that are possible, here are four that are appropriate for introducing teachers to video analysis work and that reinforce the core approaches of microethnography, noticing, and describing rather than judging. Each activity suggestion is provided with the following:

- A suggested level of prior experience in video analysis

- An overview of the activity

- The underlying design components that relate to the particular activity

- An example of the activity with specifics

- A template that can be used to implement the activity

- Optional variations or extensions to the activity

In this way, the activities can be quickly reviewed across the chapters, and those that best fit can be utilized without necessarily using them all or using them in order. In this chapter

1. The first VAT activity, *Selective Verbatim*, involves verbatim scripting in tandem with a chosen focus, in this case, teacher question types

2. The second activity, *Interactional Flow*, engages viewers in talk-mapping to explore interaction patterns in the lesson

3. The third activity, *Time Sampling*, uses time intervals to collect data around students' behavior working with partners or in a peer group

4. The fourth activity, *Tallying*, examines various uses of teacher praise

These activities are intentionally presented with fairly generic teaching behaviors so that they can serve for any grade level or content area but could also be readily adapted for use with more specific methods or approaches as a focus.

VAT Activity 1. Selective Verbatim

Level of Activity

Introductory, suitable for novice through experienced observers

Overview

This activity actually draws on three classroom observation techniques: event sampling, selective verbatim scripting, and coding. Event sampling involves the observer waiting for a selected behavior to occur and then recording every instance of it (Good & Brophy, 2000). In this activity, viewers watch a short clip looking for the selected behavior in the video (*event sampling*) and write down exact wording of the teacher or students based only on that focus (*selective verbatim scripting*). Viewers can then verify their findings with others to validate their wording. Viewers group the language they captured into predetermined categories or create their own categories (*coding*).

Underlying Design Components

- Because teachers are not asked to observe everything they see, due to the restriction of focusing only on teachers' questions, the observing task becomes more manageable.

- By asking teachers to write down the questions prior to coding them, the facilitator can ensure that what teachers code is what was said in the video.

- Since questions are a concrete observable, as opposed to something like "look for higher order thinking," it makes the viewing more reliable.

- By controlling the kinds of notes teachers can make, the possibility to wander into judgment making is curtailed, and descriptive skills like verbatim note-taking are enhanced.

- Reviewing the video multiple times contributes to teachers' appreciation of the richness of the material, as they will discover something new each time.

An Example

Step 1. The purpose for the video analysis is set. Participants are told the focus of the VAT activity is to explore questioning, which is an essential component of student thinking and student response types.

Step 2. Viewers are shown a short clip of about three minutes in which the teacher is at the front of the room leading a whole-class activity and there are a number of questions posed. (As with all of these activities, the facilitator should try the complete activity first on their own with the video clip they plan to use to ensure it will be workable for the task.) Viewers watch without taking any notes, and no discussion is allowed. They are asked to jot down their brief impressions based on that viewing. Often teachers will be quite harsh or quite complementary, and what they write is largely evaluative. This VAT task can be practiced using this video, at https://www.youtube.com/watch?v=ktRuN54CE1I, from :27 through 2:50. When using videos retrieved from online sources, make sure to begin the video analysis task after any introductory text or commentary so as not to bias the viewers. Allowing participants to watch "raw" video is essential to all of these tasks. Downloading them from their source enables facilitators to edit them or trim away text and commentary, and allows viewing without the labels or comments that might be found next to the video on the host site.

Step 3. Teachers are then asked to re-watch the same clip, writing down verbatim (word-for-word) every question they hear the teacher pose in the clip. Often this step has to be repeated a couple of times—hence the need for a short clip.

Step 4. Teachers then work with a partner or in a small group to compare what they have written down and revise their notes. It can be helpful to tell the teachers how many questions in total they should wind up with. At this point, the group usually wants the video clip to be played again.

Step 5. Teachers then share out the questions they heard while the facilitator writes them on a poster or projector, so all can see them. There will still be discrepancies about language and also about whether certain questions were really questions or more rhetorical or commands masked as questions. This can be an interesting element of the group process. The facilitator can also calculate the number of questions per minute at this point.

Step 6. Teachers then are working with the single list of questions. The facilitator provides Webb's Depth of Knowledge or Bloom's Taxonomy, and the teachers work in pairs or small groups to categorize each question as to whether it was higher or lower order.

Step 7. Teachers share out how they categorized the questions, and discussion can occur here as well, as some questions are typically hard to categorize.

Step 8. Teachers are given a chance to return to the observation statement they made in Step 1 and reflect on it as well as the entire VAT activity.

Optional Variations and Extensions

a. Teachers do this again together on another type of clip from another portion of a lesson or another grade level. Repeated sampling often results in teachers discovering similar patterns of questioning.

b. Teachers view the same clip and now note other aspects of the questioning, such as wait time following each question, who the teacher calls on to respond, or where students are sitting who are called on.

c. Teachers do this independently on their own short clip of teaching and compare their results to the group activity.

d. Additional types of qualities of questions can be examined—for example, Good and Brophy, 2000, p. 61.

e. Other categories of teacher talk that could be selected as a focus include the following: questions, directions/instruction, and feedback. Other categories of student talk could include responses to questions and student-initiated statements.

Template to Guide VAT Activity 1

Verbatim Scripting: Focus on Questioning

1. Watch the video, and without talking to anyone, write down your observations of the teacher's use of questioning seen in the clip.

2. Watch the clip again, this time writing down, word-for-word, every question you hear the teacher posing. You may need to have the clip played several times.

Questions

1.

2.

3.

And so forth . . .

3. Divide the number of questions asked by the number of minutes of the video to arrive at a question per minute ratio.

4. Match the questions that have been noted to the category on the provided higher-order thinking chart (https://static.pdesas.org/content/documents/M1-Slide_19_DOK_Wheel_Slide.pdf or https://www.cloud.edu/Assets/PDFs/assessment/revised-blooms-chart.pdf).

5. Return to your observation statement in #1 of this template. What do you think of it now? What would you revise or expand in it?

6. Reflect on this video analysis task. What do you think you learned or reinforced from participating in it?

VAT Activity 2. Interactional Flow

Level of Activity

Introductory, suitable for novice through experienced observers

Overview

This technique is similar to selective verbatim, which focuses on the content of communication. Verbal flow, however, identifies the initiators (source) and recipients (target) of the interaction and can be used with similar categories or focus areas as seen in verbatim scripting. In this activity, viewers watch a medium-length clip (six to eight minutes) and create a seating map of the classroom using boxes to represent the teacher and students. Depending on the focus area, viewers mark the seating chart with directional arrows to indicate who is speaking and to whom. Viewers can then verify their findings with others. Viewers then tally the communication directionality they have recorded.

Underlying Design Components

- Because teachers are not asked to take notes but rather to capture just who is speaking, the observing task becomes more manageable.

- Since source and target of speech is a concrete observable as opposed to something like "look for higher-order thinking," it makes the viewing more reliable.

- By avoiding any note-taking, the possibility to wander into judgment-making is curtailed and noticing skills are enhanced. Creating a visual of the classroom's interaction patterns offers a different view of classroom talk.

- When everyone is observing the same video and the facilitator stops to verify findings, there is built-in checking of one's own notes with others.

- Reviewing the video multiple times contributes to teachers' appreciation of the richness of the material, as they will discover something new each time.

An Example

Step 1. The purpose for the video analysis is set. Participants are told the focus of the VAT activity is to explore verbal/nonverbal interactions in the whole class format, which is an indicator of student involvement.

Step 2. Viewers are shown a clip (about six minutes) in which the teacher is at the front of the room leading a whole-class activity. (As with all of these activities, the facilitator should try the complete activity first on their own with the video clip they plan to use to ensure it will be workable for the task.) Viewers watch without taking any notes, and no discussion is allowed. They are asked to jot down their brief impressions based on that viewing. This VAT task can be practiced using this video, at http://tle.mivideo.it.umich.edu/media/t/0_vgq8qqnd/41959862, from minute 1:18–7:38. When using videos retrieved from online sources, make sure to begin the video analysis task after any introductory text or commentary so as not to bias the viewers. Allowing participants to watch "raw" video is essential to all of these tasks. Downloading them from their source enables facilitators to edit them or trim away text and commentary, and allows viewing without the labels or comments that might be found next to the video on the host site.

Step 3. Teachers are then asked to re-watch the same clip and create a seating map of the classroom using boxes to represent the teacher and students. When the teacher makes a comment

(Continued)

(Continued)

or asks a question to the whole class, indicate with an arrow from the teacher box. When the teacher speaks specifically to a student, indicate with a downward arrow in that student's box. When the student speaks to the teacher or the whole class, indicate with an upward arrow in that student's box. When a student speaks to another student, indicate with an arrow between the two students' boxes noting the direction. Sometimes student interactions are nonverbal gestures, such as using thumbs-up/thumbs-down or holding up a number of fingers to correspond with an answer key. Use notches on the arrows to keep track of the number of comments, gestures, or questions.

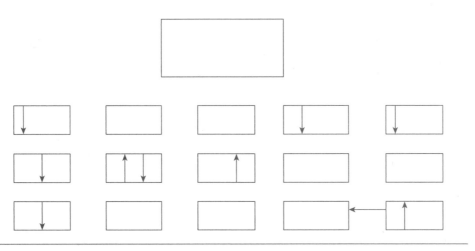

Acheson, K., & Gall, M. (1992).

Step 4. Teachers then work with a partner or in a small group to compare what they have written down and revise their notes. It can be helpful to tell the teachers approximately how many arrows in total they should wind up with. At this point, the group may want the video clip to be played again.

Step 5. The facilitator can now project their diagram for teachers to compare with their own. There will be discrepancies about the talk and gestures that they observed, and this can be an interesting element of the group process. The facilitator can then ask teachers to tally the communication observed, arriving at totals. Reflection can ensue related to the findings in terms of patterns of calling on students; considerations such as gender, volunteers, or location in the room can be discussed.

Step 6. Teachers are given a chance to return to the observation statement they made in Step 1 and reflect on it as well as the entire VAT activity.

Optional Variations and Extensions

a. Teachers do this again together on another type of clip from another portion of a lesson or another grade level. Repeated sampling often results in teachers discovering similar patterns of questioning.

b. Teachers repeat the activity using the same clip but tally some other aspect of the interaction (see Fanselow, 1987).

c. Teachers do this independently on their own short clip of teaching and compare their results to the group activity.

Template to Guide VAT Activity 2

Interactional Flow: Focus on Source and Target of Classroom Talk

1. Watch the video, and without talking to anyone, write down your observations of the classroom talk and gestures between teacher and students, students to teacher, and student to student, as seen in the clip.

2. Watch the clip again, this time creating a classroom map and marking arrows for the communication that you see occurring, as per the provided instructions.

3. Compare your results to others.

4. Consider

   • Does the teacher question or call on students sitting in parts of the room?

   • Does the teacher question or call on particular individuals or a particular gender?

   • Do particular students ask more questions or direct comments to the teacher? To other students?

5. Return to your observation statement in #1 of this template. What do you think of it now? What would you revise or expand in it?

6. Reflect on this video analysis task. What do you think you learned or reinforced from participating in it?

VAT Activity 3. Time Sampling

Level of Activity

Introductory, suitable for novice through experienced observers

Overview

In time sampling, the observer records behavior that is occurring at set intervals (Good & Brophy, 2000, p. 57). In this activity, viewers watch a video while looking at a student behavior under focus in the video every three minutes (*time sampling*) and assign the behavior to a predetermined category (*coding*). Viewers can then pool their findings with others (*multiple data sources*) to create a combined data set describing the activity.

Underlying Design Components

- Because teachers are prohibited from observing too much, due to restriction of focusing only on one learner and one behavior, the observing task becomes more manageable.

- By controlling the kinds of notes teachers can make, the possibility to wander into judgment-making is curtailed and descriptive skills are enhanced.

- When everyone is observing the same video and the facilitator stops to verify findings, there is built-in checking of one's own findings with others.

- Reviewing the video multiple times contributes to teachers' appreciation of the richness of the material, as they will discover something new each time and realize how easy it is to miss interactions in the moment.

An Example: Focus on Student Interaction in Peer Learning

Step 1. The purpose for the video analysis is set. Teachers are told the focus of this VAT activity is to explore student interaction in peer-learning tasks, linking the target of observation to student learning. Watching how students interact or behave when the teacher is not present is a way to understand how to structure such tasks and create collaborative participation norms that deepen student involvement.

Step 2. Teachers are shown a medium-length clip of about six to eight minutes in which there are pairs or a small peer group of students working independently on a task. (As with all of these activities, the facilitator should try the complete activity first on their own with the video clip they plan to use to ensure it will be workable for the task.) Viewers watch about three minutes of the clip without taking any notes, and no discussion is allowed. Viewers are asked to jot down their brief impressions about the students' behavior based on that viewing. This VAT can be practiced using this video, at https://connectedmath.msu.edu/video/grade-6-videos/student-discourse/student-discourse-chapter-4-of-7-multiplication-of-mixed-numbers/, which is about four minutes long. When using videos retrieved from online sources, make sure to begin the video analysis task after any introductory text or commentary so as not to bias the viewers. Allowing participants to watch "raw" video is essential to all of these tasks. Downloading them from their source enables facilitators to edit them or trim away text and commentary, and allows viewing without the labels or comments that might be found next to the video on the host site.

Step 3. The facilitator provides a video viewing guide, which is a pre-made menu of types of student behaviors that might be seen, and space for viewers to code the ones they observe with timestamps. The guide is discussed so that viewers are familiar with the menu prior to analyzing the video clip. This could look like the one provided after the template below.

Step 4. Teachers are then assigned a particular student seated in the pair or group on the video and asked to watch the whole clip, coding the behavior they see at set intervals, for a total of 4 or 5 timestamps. If there are five students in the group, place your viewers in groups of five and assign each of them a corresponding student in the video group; if there are three students in the group, place your viewers in groups of three, and so on. Often this step has to be repeated until viewers have the timestamps completed.

Step 5. Teachers then share their findings about their assigned student in their small group to compare what they have each coded. At this point, the group might want the video clip to be played again. The group combines their findings for each behavior, for instance, across all the viewers, "How many had timestamps for asking their partner a question?" By consolidating their findings about each student into one overall tally, the behavior of the students within the pairs or groups is arrived at since simultaneously observing every student is not possible.

Step 6. Teachers then share out their findings, and the facilitator writes them on a poster or projector so all can see them on a master-viewing guide. There may be some debate at this point about different findings. This discussion is an important part of examining the challenges of observation when the criteria are broader and the moments of note-taking vary even slightly.

Step 7. Teachers are given a chance to return to the observation statement they made in Step 1 and reflect on it as well as the entire VAT activity.

Optional Variations and Extensions

a. Teachers who work alone on this task can do so by coding each learner one by one and viewing the video multiple times, then combining the findings from each student.

b. The activity can be run as a jigsaw, with the base group each being assigned a single student in the video, sharing their findings, adjusting them, and then traveling to the visiting group to share their findings and combine them.

c. Teachers do this independently on their own short clip of teaching and compare their results to the group activity.

Template to Guide VAT Activity 3

Time Sampling: Focus on Student Interaction in Peer Learning

1. Watch the video, and without talking to anyone, write down your observations of the partner's or group's interaction.

2. Use the provided Video Viewing Guide to timestamp at two-minute intervals.

   Which student are you observing?

   1:00

   3:00

   5:00

   7:00

3. Return to your observation statement in #1 of this template. What do you think of it now? What would you revise or expand in it?

4. Reflect on this video analysis task. What do you think you learned or reinforced from participating in it? What surprised you or stood out to you after looking at this aspect of teaching in the video clip? What did this observation task make you think of changing in your own teaching?

VAT Activity 4. Tallying

Level of Activity

Introductory, suitable for novice through experienced observers

Overview

In this activity, teachers watch a segment of video looking for particular activities and do not take notes but rather tally instances of the activity by the teacher or students in a provided table of predetermined categories, based on the work of Flanders (1970). Viewers then verify their findings with others.

Underlying Design Components

- Because teachers are prohibited from observing too much, due to restriction of focusing only on one target, the observing task becomes more manageable.

- Since the viewer only has to make a tally mark in a predetermined category, the viewer's guide itself serves a kind of professional-learning function, exposing the viewers to the many ways something as narrow as praise can actually be implemented.

- By controlling the kinds of notes teachers can make, the possibility to wander into judgment-making is curtailed and descriptive skills like tallying are enhanced.

- When everyone is observing the same video and the facilitator stops to verify findings, there is built-in checking of one's own findings with others.

- Reviewing the video multiple times contributes to teachers' appreciation of the richness of the material as they will discover something new each time and realize how easy it is to miss interactions in the moment.

An Example

Step 1. The purpose for the video analysis is set. Teachers are told the focus of this VAT activity is to explore teachers' use of praise, linking the target of observation to student learning. For instance, creating a positive classroom climate is a way teachers generate student involvement. Teachers' use of praise is one aspect of positive classroom climate.

Step 2. Teachers are shown a short clip of about five minutes in which there are a number of instances of praise, captured perhaps during a share-out component of the lesson. (As with all of these activities, the facilitator should try the complete activity first on their own with the video clip they plan to use to ensure it will be workable for the task.) They watch without taking any notes, and no discussion is allowed. Viewers are asked to jot down their brief impressions about the teacher's use of praise based on that viewing. This VAT can be practiced using this video, at https://www.youtube.com/watch?v=yAdx2--3lZ0, which is about two and half minutes long. When using videos retrieved from online sources, make sure to begin the video analysis task after any introductory text or commentary so as not to bias the viewers. Allowing participants to watch "raw" video is essential to all of these tasks. Downloading them from their source enables facilitators to edit them or trim away text and commentary and allows viewing without the labels or comments that might be found next to the video on the host site.

Step 3. The facilitator provides a video-viewing guide, which is a pre-made table with types of praise and space for viewers to code the ones they hear with tally marks. The guide is reviewed

(Continued)

(Continued)

so that viewers are familiar with the categories and examples prior to analyzing the video clip. This could look like the one provided after the Template to Guide VAT Activity 2 below.

Step 4. Teachers are then asked to re-watch the same clip, coding the praise they hear on the viewing guide. Often this step has to be repeated a couple of times—hence the need for a short clip. Viewers can be encouraged to code five instances of praise.

Step 5. Teachers then work with a partner or in a small group to compare what they have each tallied. At this point, the group might want the video clip to be played again.

Step 6. Teachers then share out the tallies they made, and the facilitator writes them on a poster or projector so all can see them on a master viewing guide. There may be some debate at this point about how certain instances of praise should be coded. This discussion is an important part of examining this aspect of teaching.

Step 7. Teachers are given a chance to return to the observation statement they made in Step 1 and reflect on it as well as the entire VAT activity.

Optional Variations and Extensions

a. Teachers do this again in an online activity that provides the facilitator's tally marks once the teacher has submitted theirs. Repeated sampling often results in teachers discovering similar patterns of the use of praise.

b. Teachers view the same clip and now note other aspects of the use of praise, such as who the teacher gives the praise to or where students are sitting who receive it.

c. Teachers do this independently on their own short clip of teaching and compare their results to the group activity.

Template to Guide VAT Activity 4

Tallying: Focus on Praise

1. Watch the video, and without talking to anyone, write down your observations of the teacher's use of praise as seen in the clip.

2. Use the provided video viewing guide to tally at least five instances of praise that you hear during the video playback. Jot notes if possible about each one.

3. Return to your observation statement in #1 of this template. What do you think of it now? What would you revise or expand in it?

4. Reflect on this video analysis task. What do you think you learned or reinforced from participating in it? What surprised you or stood out to you after looking at this aspect of teaching in the video clip? What did this observation task make you think of changing in your own teaching?

Video Viewing Guide: Investigating the Use of Praise

View the following video clip and, using the instrument below, note each instance of teacher praise that you hear. Then, check off all the aspects of that praise that apply. An example is provided.

Categories of Praise	
Vague (Super!)	√ "Great work today!"
Specific (You added a lot of interesting details)	
Perseverance (worked long and hard)	

(Continued)

(Continued)

Categories of Praise	
Effort (trying, guessing, suggesting)	
Progress (relative to past)	
Success (right answer)	
Originality (imagination, creativity)	
Neatness (careful work)	
Obedience (follows rules, pays attention, compliant)	
Prosocial behavior (courtesy, thoughtfulness)	
Other purposes (specify)	

PUTTING IDEAS INTO ACTION

Looking across the ideas and activities presented in this chapter, consider the following questions:

1. What do you see as common features across all four video analysis activities in this chapter?

2. What skills for video viewing might teachers develop if they completed these activities?

3. What do you anticipate as problematic, new, or uncomfortable if you were trying these activities out with teachers?

4. In what ways could these activities be set up in an online, self-paced format?

5. Which parts of this chapter resonate for you in terms of facilitating teachers' conversations or for your own use of video analysis?

Chapter References

Acheson, K. & Gall, M. (1992). *Techniques in the clinical supervision of teachers* (2nd ed.). New York: Longman.

Fanselow, J. F. (1987). *Breaking rules: Generating and exploring alternatives in language teaching.* New York, NY: Longman.

Flanders, N. A. (1970). *Analyzing teaching behavior.* Reading, MA: Addison-Wesley.

Good, T. L., & Brophy, J. E. (2000). *Looking in classrooms* (8th ed.). New York, NY: Longman.

Hellermann, J., & Jakonen, T. (2015). Interactional approaches to the study of classroom discourse and student learning. In K. King, Y.J. Lai, & S. May (Eds.), *Research Methods in Language and Education* (pp. 1–13). New York, NY: Springer International Publishing.

Hornberger, N. H. (1995). Ethnography in linguistic perspective: Understanding school processes 1. *Language and education, 9*(4), 233–248.

Streeck, J., & Mehus, S. (2005). Micro-ethnography: The study of practices. In K. Fitch & R. Sanders (Eds.), *Handbook of language and social interaction* (pp. 381–404). Mahwah, NJ: Lawrence Erlbaum.

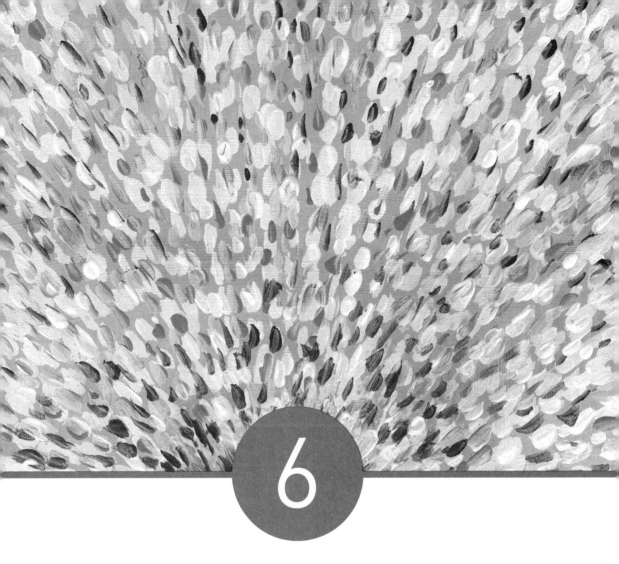

6

VIDEO USED TO EXPLORE
DILEMMAS OF PRACTICE

In a dilemma, it is helpful to change any variable,
then reexamine the problem.

—Robert A. Heinlein, *Have Space Suit—Will Travel*

CHAPTER OBJECTIVES

- To present teaching dilemmas as an organizing frame for video analysis of teaching

- To offer suggestions about how to view video as an artifact used along with existing analytic protocols

- To outline approaches that invite teachers to share findings across multiple or single videos and from different points of view

In the first part of this book as well as in Chapter 5, the importance of sensitivity to teachers' vulnerabilities and the need to begin video analysis upon a solid, shared foundation of careful, nonevaluative observational skills was presented. This chapter assumes that those introductory experiences have been successfully introduced and that teachers are now ready to go further in their application of video analysis. In addition, the activities presented lend themselves to scaling up teacher professional learning at a group or course level. Detailed descriptions of four approaches that are easily adapted to specific pedagogical foci are offered, which can be used to introduce teachers to video analysis in ways that still rely on a high degree of structure but could also become less structured depending on the level of the experience of the participants.

DILEMMAS OF PRACTICE AS AN APPROACH FOR EXPLORING TEACHING

Teachers who have become more skilled at carefully avoiding judgment while observing narrowly focused classroom interactions are ready to tackle more complex dilemmas using video analysis of teaching. Dilemmas of practice are complex situations for which there are no "right" or "wrong" answers and to which teachers will respond differently and in accordance with the particulars of the context. Unlike problems that are cleanly resolved, dilemmas leave a sense of concern or discontent for the practitioner, which makes these situations complicated when teachers have to make these decisions on their own (Berlak & Berlak, 1981; Denicolo, 1996).

Teaching, in particular, is usually carried out in isolation and yet is a highly decision-driven activity. It also takes place in unpredictable environments with multiple players, which make it particularly dilemmatic in nature (Cabaroglu & Tillema, 2011). In short, every day teachers must face dilemmas, and while they cannot avoid them, "they can find various strategies for handling [them], which are shaped by teachers' values, priorities, knowledge, and their awareness and ability to reflect on alternatives" (Scager, Akkerman, Pilot, & Wubbels, 2017, p. 319).

Video analysis is well suited to the exploration of classroom dilemmas, as through shared video review, teachers' isolation or even embarrassment is reduced—they can engage in collaborative conversations about particularly troubling or aggravating aspects of their practice and thus reduce their sense of being alone in their struggles. When descriptive observation is employed in exploring particular dilemmas, teachers often realize that what they perceived to be unsuccessful may have indeed been working just fine according to other viewers. They can also begin to identify, as the Heinlein quote above suggests, those particular moves or talk that could be altered, potentially leading to different results and even resolution of the dilemma under study.

USING VIDEO ANALYSIS OF TEACHING TO EXPLORE DILEMMAS OF PRACTICE

While there are many types of video analysis of teaching (VAT) activities that are possible, here are four which are appropriate for introducing or continuing to build teachers' understanding of classrooms through video analysis work. These activities are designed to reinforce the core approaches of microethnography (describing rather than judging) and praxis (developing theory from practice and developing practice from theory). These video analysis activities can also be directed to target specific dilemmas that teachers perceive are of concern. Each activity suggestion is provided with

- A suggested level of prior experience in video analysis
- An overview of the activity
- The underlying design components that relate to the particular activity
- An example of the activity with specifics
- A template that can be used to implement the activity
- Optional variations or extensions to the activity

In this way, the activities can be quickly reviewed across the chapters, and those that best fit can be utilized without necessarily using them all or using them in order. In this chapter, four VAT activities are presented:

1. *Virtual grand rounds* ➜ Video clips are used to spark a focused investigation of a particular practice across several classrooms.

2. *Conversation analysis* ➜ Segments of video related to classroom talk are transcribed and examined for deeper student and teacher roles.

3. *Student perspective video* ➜ Students wear a mounted video camera and footage from their point of view is captured, and student reflections are incorporated into the video analysis process.

4. *Student work samples with video records* ➜ Both video clips and student work from the same lesson are reviewed together for deeper insights into student learning.

These activities are intentionally presented with fairly generic teaching behaviors so that they can serve for any grade level or content area and can be readily adapted for use with more specific methods or approaches as a focus.

VAT Activity 1. Virtual Grand Rounds

Level of Activity

Introductory, suitable for novice through experienced observers

Overview

When educators are focused on better understanding a particular dilemma in their practice—classroom management issues, for instance—an instructional round can build greater understanding of the issue across a group of educators. The term "instructional rounds" is taken from the terminology used in the medical profession, in which a lead physician "rounds" through problems presented in the form of patient cases, trailed by residents who benefit from the leader's insights (Roegman & Riehl, 2012). In education, instructional rounds involve a facilitator who is an expert educator leading others in their observation and analysis of teaching (Troen & Boles, 2014). Due to the barriers of time and location, it can be very difficult to schedule instructional rounds within a single school, much less across multiple schools. For student teachers in teacher education programs, this type of rounding can be impossible to set up. This is where the "virtual" of "virtual grand rounds" can be of use.

Virtual grand rounds have been shown to be a highly effective way to support larger groups of educators in exploring particular aspects of teaching using video records rather than going to observe live (Cuthrell, Steadman, Stapleton, & Hodge, 2016). This activity could draw on any variety of classroom observation techniques introduced in Chapter 5, such as event sampling, selective verbatim scripting, and/or coding. It is best begun with a common base video, then inviting participants to observe several more "cases" of the issue under study, either by providing preselected video clips or by inviting participants to review their own video clips specifically keyed to the dilemma under study.

Underlying Design Components

- When teachers are asked to observe one aspect of classroom practice rather than noticing everything in the video, the observing task becomes more manageable.

- By asking teachers to share and review a base video that represents the dilemma of practice together first, viewing norms are established and teachers' follow-up observations can become more reliable and valid.

- Within a specific dilemma of practice as the focus, such as "giving instructions," teachers can break it down and utilize a number of observational practices to make as much sense of the practice as possible. For instance, they can look at the language used, the teacher's body language, and students' behaviors to try to understand the dilemma.

- By controlling the kinds of notes teachers can make, the possibility of wandering into exploring other dilemmas of practice is curtailed.

An Example

Step 1. The purpose for the video analysis is set. Participants are told the focus of the VAT activity is to explore a dilemma teachers are having around giving instructions, which is an essential component of classroom management.

Step 2. Viewers are shown a short clip of about three to five minutes in which the teacher is giving instructions and both the teacher and the students are visible on the video. (As with all of these activities, the facilitator should try the complete activity first on their own with the video clip they plan to use to ensure it will be workable for the task.) Viewers watch without taking any notes, and no discussion is allowed. They are asked to jot down their brief impressions based on that viewing. Half of the viewers could be told that they are the teacher's coach and that the teacher has been struggling with giving instructions in ways that are effective, while the other half is told that the teacher is excellent at instruction-giving. Assign these roles secretly. While they watch, observers can jot down notes on anything they wish. The rationale for this is to sensitize participants to the powerful influence of bias when moving from discrete observation tasks to more open-ended ones. This VAT can be practiced using this video, at https://www.youtube.com/watch?v=kTU9gv4LiHc, which is a little over two minutes long. When using videos retrieved from online sources, make sure to begin the video analysis task after any introductory text or commentary so as not to bias the viewers. Allowing participants to watch "raw" video is essential to all of these tasks. Downloading them from their source enables facilitators to edit them or trim away text and commentary and allows viewing without the labels or comments that might be found next to the video on the host site.

Step 3. Teachers are then asked to re-watch the same clip, writing down everything about the teacher's instructions that they believe is taking place during the instruction-giving. Often this step has to be repeated a couple of times—hence the need for a short clip.

Step 4. Teachers then work with a partner or in a small group with others who had the opposite "coach" role, to compare what they have written down and revise their notes. This helps in creating a shared sense of what it means to give "effective" instructions. Often when we are biased before viewing, we see only certain aspects and ignore others. This is like the doctor, who on doing her rounds believes the patient has a particular illness and then seeks out those symptoms that support her belief rather than the other way around. Language from a teacher–observation rubric on giving instructions could be offered to the group at this stage to spark further consideration of what took place in the video as "effective" or "not-effective," such as https://www.kean.edu/~tpc/Classroom%20 Management/EFFECTIVE%20LESSON%20PLANNING%20&%20Classroom%20Mgmt.htm.

Step 5. Teachers then share out their findings to the whole group, and the facilitator can try to create a master list of observables in "effective" versus "less-effective" instruction-giving, in the spirit of supporting this teacher in exploring this particular problem of practice. The facilitator can help participants grasp the importance of letting go of judgment before being able to "see" more objectively. The group can come up with those observables that really seem to help make the instruction-giving achieve its purpose, along with generating alternatives that were not seen in the clip.

Step 6. Teachers then move on to observe three to five other example clips of instruction-giving to further explore their understanding of instruction-giving. They can add to the shared master list as they go. This can be done with shared, commonly viewed additional video clips, or this could be done privately with teachers visiting each other's classrooms or viewing other videos on their own and returning to the group with their findings.

Step 7. Teachers are given a chance to return to the observation statement they made in Step 1 and reflect on it as well as the entire VAT activity.

Optional Variations and Extensions

a. Teachers observe for the same qualities of instruction-giving across multiple grade levels. Repeated sampling often results in teachers discovering similar patterns as well as important differences.

b. Teachers are provided video clips predetermined to have highly effective instruction-giving, using the criteria developed in the session to justify their observation.

c. Teachers do this independently on their own short clip of teaching and compare their results to the group activity, with the facilitator helping the viewers to come to appropriate conclusions and questioning their judgments.

d. Additional qualities of classroom management can be examined by seeking out observation protocols available online or in the local context.

e. Other categories of classroom management that could be selected as a focus include the following: Openings/Closings, Transitions, and Materials Distribution.

Template to Guide VAT Activity

Virtual Grand Rounds: Focus on Giving Instructions

1. Watch the video, and without talking to anyone, write down your observations of the teacher's instruction-giving as seen in the clip. Observe from the point of view of the role your facilitator has assigned you.

2. Watch the clip again, this time writing down as much as you can related to the teacher's instruction-giving.

3. Share your findings with a partner or small group who had the opposite role from you. How do checklists for "effective" instruction-giving inform—or direct—your observation?

   This is an example of giving instructions from an observation checklist:

   Begin lessons by giving clear instructions:

   a. *State desired quality of work.*

   b. *Have students paraphrase directions.*

   c. *Ensure that everyone is paying attention.*

   d. *Ensure that all distractions have been removed.*

   e. *Describe expectations, activities, and evaluation procedures.*

   Partial list retrieved from http://www.kean.edu/~tpc/Classroom%20Management/ EFFECTIVE%20LESSON%20PLANNING%20&%20Classroom%20Mgmt.htm

4. Share your findings with the whole group, coming up with a set of observables that you believe can justify whether instruction-giving appeared to be effective. Then, go out to other classrooms or observe other videos or video yourself, focusing just on instruction-giving. What did you discover?

5. Return to your observation statement in #1 of this template. What do you think of it now? What would you revise or expand in it?

6. Reflect on this video analysis task. What do you think you learned or reinforced from participating in it?

VAT Activity 2. Conversation Analysis

Level of Activity

Intermediate, suitable for observers with some prior experience

Overview

Conversation analysis is a widely used method in qualitative research, and it is applied in a similar way to video analysis of teaching in this activity. It involves verbatim transcription of talk, which is then coded according to the lens of the investigator. When educators are focused on a dilemma of practice, conversation analysis, while time-consuming and intensive, can be a very powerful opportunity to gain surprising insights into practice. This approach is particularly effective for creating dissonance between how teachers might believe they are behaving and their actual behavior. For instance, when teachers are hoping to draw out students' ideas and encourage them to extend their talk but are frustrated by the lack of such conversation in class, it can be helpful to zoom in and closely examine classroom interaction.

In their work with teachers attempting to foster difficult conversations about race in their classrooms, Vetter and Schieble (2015) note that video analysis is conducive to examining the identity the teacher wishes to have vis-à-vis students and the positions they actually take up in moment-to-moment classroom interactions. In their work, they found that teachers began to better understand why, in some cases, students were not forthcoming or did not elaborate on their opinions, once they saw the language, both verbal and nonverbal, they were inadvertently using while leading classroom discussions. Use of conversation analysis with video review is very useful when exploring subtle, complex dilemmas of teaching.

Underlying Design Components

- Capturing the actual speech that occurs can force viewers to rewind and review many times and bring awareness of the importance of word choice, language use, and nonverbal signals in their classroom interactions.

- When everyone is observing the same video and the facilitator stops to verify findings, there is built-in checking of one's own notes with others.

- Reviewing the video multiple times contributes to teachers' appreciation of the richness of the material, as they will discover something new each time.

An Example

Step 1. The purpose for the video analysis is set. Participants are told the focus of the VAT activity is to explore discussion techniques. The teacher's dilemma is that she wishes for a greater amount of student discussion.

Step 2. Viewers are shown a short clip of about five minutes in which the teacher is leading a whole-class discussion. (As with all of these activities, the facilitator should try the complete activity first on their own with the video clip they plan to use to ensure it will be workable for the task.) Viewers watch without taking any notes, and no discussion is allowed. They are asked to jot down their brief impressions based on that viewing. This VAT can be practiced using this video, at https://achievethecore.org/page/2877/using-complex-text-to-build-content-knowledge-motter, from 44:00 through 48:00, which is about four minutes long. When using videos retrieved from online sources, make sure to begin the video analysis task after any introductory text or

(Continued)

(Continued)

commentary so as not to bias the viewers. Allowing participants to watch "raw" video is essential to all of these tasks. Downloading them from their source enables facilitators to edit them or trim away text and commentary, and allows viewing without the labels or comments that might be found next to the video on the host site.

Step 3. Teachers are then asked to re-watch the same clip and capture the exact language from the clip. Pairs can be matched so one person captures all the teacher's talk, and the other partner, all the students' talk. They can then co-construct the dialogue. At this point, the group may want the video clip to be played again.

Step 4. Teachers then are provided with the actual transcript that the facilitator has prepared, and they check for discrepancies. There usually are some, and this can be an interesting point of discussion. Often our brains are wired to "fill in the blanks," and we can become more present and aware when we realize we do not hear everything.

Step 5. The facilitator can now ask the participants in pairs or groups to label the "language functions" of the talk they have down in the transcript. Possible functions are provided, such as questioning, persuading, informing, and so forth. Once these are labeled or in discussion of how they should be labeled, an analysis of the discussion can take place. Participants can consider how the functions taken up by the teacher and students' language act as clues as to how the classroom discussion could be deepened.

Step 6. Teachers are given a chance to return to the observation statement they made in Step 1 and reflect on it as well as the entire VAT activity.

Optional Variations and Extensions

a. Teachers do this again together on another type of clip from another portion of a lesson or another grade level. Repeated sampling often results in teachers discovering similar patterns.

b. Teachers review the transcript but with another focus for their analysis.

c. Teachers do this independently on their own short clip of teaching and compare their results to the group activity.

Template to Guide VAT Activity

Conversation Analysis: Focus on Classroom Discussion

1. Watch the video, and without talking to anyone, write down your observations of the classroom discussion, as seen in the clip.

2. Watch the clip again, this time writing down the exact talk you heard, perhaps sharing the transcription writing with a partner.

3. Compare your results to the transcript provided by the facilitator. Consider why there were discrepancies.

4. Label the talk in the transcript according to a provided list of language functions. How does this help you understand the nature of the discussion? Possible functions include the following:

    - Seek Information
    - Inform
    - Compare
    - Classify
    - Justify
    - Infer
    - Evaluate

5. Return to your observation statement in #1 of this template. What do you think of it now? What would you revise or expand in it?

6. Reflect on this video analysis task. What do you think you learned or reinforced from participating in it?

VAT Activity 3. Student Perspective Video

Level of Activity

Intermediate, suitable for observers with some prior experience

Overview

In this activity, viewers watch a video in order to focus on the student's point of view. This kind of video is captured by placing a camera close to a student or students during their think-alouds during class. For a very specific example of this, in Estapa, Pinnow, and Chval's (2016) study, they researched the insights teachers gained by actually attaching a small video camera, like a GoPro, to a baseball hat and having students wear it to capture the lesson from their point of view. In their study, this enabled a group of mathematics teachers to better perceive how an English language learner student was navigating through a math activity by giving teachers access they could never have without the video review from that angle. This is particularly important for noticing student thinking, when "teachers must decenter from their own perspective and imagine the perspective of the students" (Estapa, Pinnow, & Chval, 2016, p. 87). As in the image below, this can also be done by setting up a camera on a low tripod right behind a student at work.

Examining video footage taken from the student's point of view can be effective in addressing the tendency to attend to the teacher's actions rather than the learner's when analyzing video (Sherin & Han, 2004). Whether the dilemma of practice centers on curriculum, instruction, or individual student's behavior, observing a lesson from a single student's point of view can be eye-opening for teachers. Over a two-year period in using video taken from this angle, Estapa, Pinnow, and Chval found that "the head-mounted cameras used in the intervention provided a unique perspective of ELLs and this perspective, once viewed on video by the teachers in the study, supported a change in teacher noticing. In other words, the use of these specific video cameras influenced their understandings of what was happening in their classrooms" (2016, p. 99).

Underlying Design Components

- When teachers are asked to focus only on one learner, the observing task becomes more manageable.

- By controlling the kinds of notes teachers can make, the possibility to wander into judgment-making is curtailed and descriptive skills are enhanced.

- When everyone is observing the same video and the facilitator stops to verify findings, there is built-in checking of one's own findings with others.

- Reviewing the video multiple times contributes to teachers' appreciation of the richness of the material, as they will discover something new each time and realize how easy it is to miss interactions in the moment.

An Example: Focus on Student Thinking

Step 1. The purpose for the video analysis is set. Teachers are told the focus of this VAT activity is to explore student thinking during a learning task. Watching how students verbalize their thinking aloud or perform a task is a way to understand how to create scaffolds to address students' misconceptions and extend their thinking.

Teachers are shown a medium-length clip of about six minutes in which there is a student working on a task and expressing their reasoning aloud. This often can be found in a one-on-one episode where a teacher is asking a student to make predictions or to explain their thinking. (As with all of these activities, the facilitator should try the complete activity first on their own with the video clip they plan to use to ensure it will be appropriate.) Viewers initially watch the clip without taking any notes, and no discussion is allowed. Viewers are asked to jot down their brief impressions about the student's thinking based on that viewing. This VAT task can be practiced using this video, at https://www.youtube.com/watch?v=xyuL7W1E_9E , which is three minutes long. When using videos retrieved from online sources, make sure to begin the video analysis task after any introductory text or commentary so as not to bias the viewers. Allowing participants to watch "raw" video is essential to all of these tasks. Downloading them from their source enables facilitators to edit them or trim away text and commentary, and allows viewing without the labels or comments that might be found next to the video on the host site.

Step 2. The facilitator asks viewers to provide their observations in the frame provided on the observation template. These prompts ask teachers to review the clip and consider the student's thinking about content, the skills they are using, and what could be changed to support the student's thinking based on the evidence provided in the clip.

Step 3. Teachers then share out the observations they made, and the facilitator writes them on a poster or projector, so all can see them on a master viewing guide. There may be some debate at this point about what evidence teachers believe point to certain aspects of student thinking. This discussion should be encouraged and different conclusions might be drawn based on the evidence. At this point, the group might want the video clip to be played again.

Step 4. Teachers are given a chance to return to the observation statement they made in Step 1 and reflect on it as well as the entire VAT activity.

Optional Variations and Extensions

a. Teachers can view footage taken from several different students from the same lesson, to heighten their appreciation of how differently each learner can experience the same instruction.

b. The activity can be enhanced with the addition of student work products and the lesson plan and other learning materials that were utilized.

c. Teachers then video a one-to-one session with the particular learner, to target the particular aspects of practice they wanted to improve on in order to support student thinking.

Template to Guide VAT Activity

Student Perspective Video: Focus on Student Thinking

1. Watch the video, and without talking to anyone, write down your observations of what you believe the student is thinking during this learning task.

2. Map your observation of this student's thinking along the following points:

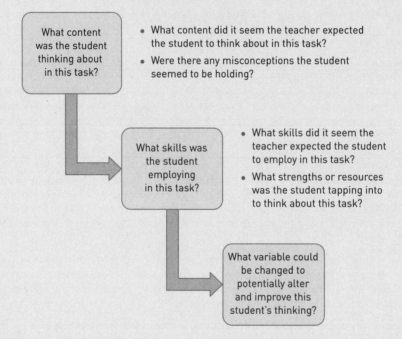

What content was the student thinking about in this task?

- What content did it seem the teacher expected the student to think about in this task?
- Were there any misconceptions the student seemed to be holding?

What skills was the student employing in this task?

- What skills did it seem the teacher expected the student to employ in this task?
- What strengths or resources was the student tapping into to think about this task?

What variable could be changed to potentially alter and improve this student's thinking?

3. Share your findings with the group.

4. Return to your observation statement in #1 of this template. What do you think of it now? What would you revise or expand in it?

5. Reflect on this video analysis task. What do you think you learned or reinforced from participating in it? What surprised you or stood out to you after looking at this aspect of teaching in the video clip? What did this observation task make you think of changing in your own teaching?

VAT Activity 4. Student Work With Video Analysis

Level of Activity

Intermediate, suitable for novice through experienced observers

Overview

Student work is another vantage point from which teachers can gain insights into students' understanding of concepts and their application of skills. Thoughtful, descriptive reflection on student work, especially in concert with other educators, is supportive of instructional decision-making for improving student learning. The success of this process depends on a shared commitment to collaboration and reflective practice. Student work artifacts, like video records, become materials that can ground conversations about teaching, curriculum, and student learning. These can be presented either with student names or with names removed and shared by teachers from their own classrooms or simply provided as samples to spark discussion.

Using a structured protocol supports targeted attention to a particular dilemma of practice and ensures that the collaborative process supports teachers' meaning-making. One that is widely used comes from the National School Reform Faculty (NSRF): (https://schoolreforminitiative.org/doc/atlas_lfsw.pdf). In fact, this protocol states that "ambiguous or puzzling work tends to stimulate the best discussions. Since it does not readily match expectations, it encourages close attention to details and affords multiple interpretations" (para. #2). These student work samples can therefore be a tangible representation of a teacher's dilemma of practice and, coupled with the video record of the lesson from which the student work is generated, can lead to even deeper understandings than either student work samples or video records alone.

Underlying Design Components

- Because teachers follow a strict protocol of turn-taking in discussing evidence from the student work and the video, the conversation stays focused.

- Maintaining the same investigative stance toward student work and video around the same focus brings awareness to how instruction and assessment are interwoven.

- By controlling the kinds of notes teachers can make and the timeframe around note-taking and discussion, the possibility to wander into judgment-making is curtailed and descriptive skills are enhanced.

- When everyone is observing the same video and student work and the facilitator stops to verify findings, there is built-in checking of one's own findings with others.

An Example

Step 1. The purpose for the video analysis is set. Teachers are told the focus of this VAT activity is to explore teacher modeling, linking the target of observation to student learning. For instance, clear modeling can support students' performance on the assigned task. By seeing the instruction as well as the outcome of that instruction in the form of the student work samples, any dilemmas around this practice can be explored.

Step 2. Teachers are given unique, different student work samples—but all pulled from the same lesson—and shown a clip of about 10 minutes from this lesson where the assignment was modeled. (As with all of these activities, the facilitator should try the complete activity first on their own with the video clip they plan to use to ensure it will be workable for the task.) Viewers are

(Continued)

(Continued)

asked to jot down their brief impressions about the teacher's modeling based on that viewing. This VAT task can be practiced using this video, at https://www.youtube.com/watch?v=QE9YbeCkLeQ, which is about ten minutes long. When using videos retrieved from online sources, make sure to begin the video analysis task after any introductory text or commentary so as not to bias the viewers. Allowing participants to watch "raw" video is essential to all of these tasks. Downloading them from their source enables facilitators to edit them or trim away text and commentary, and allows viewing without the labels or comments that might be found next to the video on the host site. Student work that could be used in association with this video would be those that feature samples of annotation, the focus of this particular video of modeling.

Step 3. Teachers then work with a small group to compare what they have each tallied, completing the parallel chart for the student work sample and the video record. This discussion could follow the parameters of the student work protocol process wherein each person contributes but within a set time frame.

Step 4. Teachers are given a chance to reflect on the entire VAT activity.

Optional Variations and Extensions

a. Teachers do this again using a different student work sample. How does looking for the same aspect of practice—modeling—but different student work samples as evidence, change teachers' findings?

b. Teachers view the same clip and now note other aspects of teaching but review the same work samples.

c. Teachers do this independently on their own short clip of teaching and student work samples and compare their results to the group activity.

Template to Guide VAT

Student Work With Video Review: Focus on Teacher Modeling

1. Watch the video, and without talking to anyone, write down your observations of the teacher's modeling in setting up an in-class assignment.

2. Examine the student work sample provided that came from this particular class. Each member of the group has a different student work sample from this observed class. Without talking to anyone, write down any connections you can see between the teacher's modeling in setting up an in-class assignment and the student work sample you are reviewing.

3. Reflecting on the student work sample and the video record:

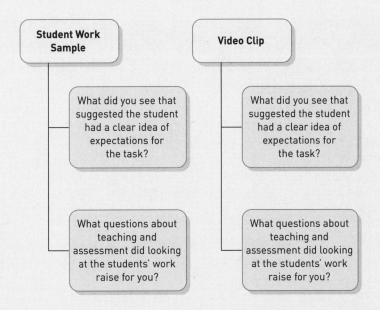

Student Work Sample	Video Clip
What did you see that suggested the student had a clear idea of expectations for the task?	What did you see that suggested the student had a clear idea of expectations for the task?
What questions about teaching and assessment did looking at the students' work raise for you?	What questions about teaching and assessment did looking at the students' work raise for you?

4. Reflect on this video analysis task. What do you think you learned or reinforced from participating in it? What surprised you or stood out to you after looking at this aspect of teaching in the student work and in the video clip? What did this observation task make you think of changing in your own teaching?

PUTTING IDEAS INTO ACTION

Looking across the ideas and activities presented in this chapter, consider the following questions:

1. What do you see as common features across all four video analysis activities in this chapter?

2. What skills for video viewing might teachers develop if they completed these activities?

3. What teaching skills might teachers develop if they completed these activities?

4. What do you anticipate as problematic, new, or uncomfortable if you were trying these activities out with teachers?

5. In what ways could these activities be set up in an online, self-paced format?

6. Which parts of this chapter resonate for you in terms of facilitating other teachers' conversations or for your own use of video analysis?

Chapter References

Berlak, A., & Berlak, H. (1981). *Dilemmas of schooling: Teaching and social change*. New York, NY: Methuen.

Cabaroglu, N., & Tillema, H. (2011). Teacher educator dilemmas: A concept to study pedagogy. *Teachers and Teaching: Theory and Practice, 17*(5), 559–573.

Cuthrell, K., Steadman, S. C., Stapleton, J., & Hodge, E. (2016). Developing expertise: Using video to hone teacher candidates' classroom observation skills. *The New Educator, 12*(1), 5–27.

Denicolo, P. (1996). Productively confronting dilemmas in educational practice and research. In M. Kompf, R. Bond, D. Dworet, & T. Boak (Eds.), *Changing research and practice: Teachers' professionalism, identities and knowledge* (pp. 56–65). London, United Kingdom: Falmer Press.

Estapa, A., Pinnow, R., & Chval, K. (2016). Video as a professional development tool to support novice teachers as they learn to teach English

language learners. *The New Educator, 12*(1), 85–104.

Roegman, R., & Riehl, C. (2012). Playing doctor with education: Considerations in using medical rounds as a model for instructional rounds. *Journal of School Leadership, 22*(5), 922–952.

Scager, K., Akkerman, S. F., Pilot, A., & Wubbels, T. (2017). Teacher dilemmas in challenging students in higher education. *Teaching in Higher Education, 22*(3), 318–335.

Sherin, M. G., & Han, S. Y. (2004). Teacher learning in the context of a video club. *Teaching and Teacher Education, 20*(2), 163–183.

Troen, V., & Boles, K. C. (2014). *The power of teacher rounds: A guide for facilitators, principals, and department chairs*. Thousand Oaks, CA: Corwin.

Vetter, A., & Schieble, M. (2015). *Observing teacher identities through video analysis: Practice and implications*. New York, NY: Routledge.

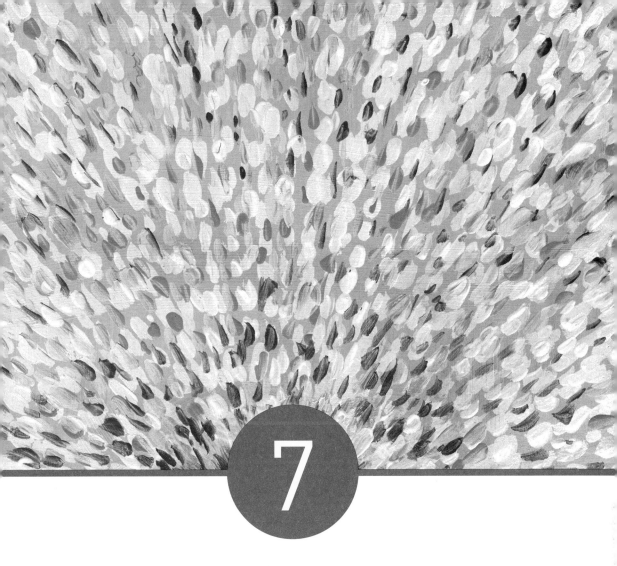

VIDEO USED TO BUILD A SHARED PROFESSIONAL VISION

Few, if any, forces in human affairs are as
powerful as shared vision.

—Peter Senge, *The Fifth Discipline: The Art and
Practice of the Learning Organization* (1990)

CHAPTER OBJECTIVES

- To emphasize the need for a shared professional vision in communities of practice
- To highlight how video analysis can support teachers' professional vision
- To outline approaches in video analysis that promote professional vision in teacher learning

This chapter continues from the introduction of low-inference, careful observation as presented in Chapter 2 and the more interpretive type of viewing tasks in Chapter 6. When teachers come together in professional-learning communities, video analysis is very effective in advancing their shared understanding of teaching and learning. In this chapter, detailed descriptions of four adaptable approaches are offered, which are each powerful learning experiences that lend themselves to strengthening teachers' professional knowledge and skills and refining their thinking about practice.

PROFESSIONAL VISION IN A TEACHER COMMUNITY OF PRACTICE

The Senge quote that opens this chapter on the power of a shared vision is written with the business community in mind, yet it could not be truer for the school setting. As DuFour (2007) puts it, "one traditional obstacle to schools' moving forward is the fact that there is an inherent tradition of teacher isolation in schools. And it has to be addressed and overcome if a school's going to become a collaborative learning community." The structures of schooling lead to teachers doing much of their observation of learning, of themselves, and of practice on their own. The benefits of sharing that work in a community of other educators are numerous; one in particular is the possibility of teachers deepening their personal as well as a shared professional vision.

Professional vision refers to how teachers use their knowledge of teaching, of their subject matter, of their learners—to arrive at decision-making in moment-to-moment classroom interactions. "Professional vision involves the ability to notice and interpret significant interactions in a classroom" (Sherin, Russ, Sherin, & Colestock, 2008, p. 28) and is both improved by and serves as the currency of meaningful interchange among teachers. When teachers engage in a community of colleagues to discuss, analyze, and reflect on instructional practices, they are able to work toward developing their personal professional vision as well as a shared professional vision—a common understanding of what effective practice looks like and what the community is striving for.

USING VIDEO ANALYSIS TO DEEPEN TEACHERS' PROFESSIONAL VISION

Video analysis is an ideal approach in working with teachers toward developing a shared professional vision. First, it offers a solution to the challenge of logistically enabling groups of teachers to routinely visit one another's classrooms and to the difficulty of having discussions immediately afterward while the memories of what was seen are still intact. In addition, particular video-recorded episodes can be selected to purposefully fuel discussion that is critical in the formation of professional vision rather than relying on the chance situations that will arise in a live observation. As discussed in Chapter 1, research has consistently shown that video is a material that is uniquely capable of offering teachers the opportunity for detailed analysis of their own classroom events while providing the distance to make new discoveries and push their thinking.

While there are many types of video analysis activities that are possible, here are four that are appropriate for introducing or continuing to build teachers' professional vision. These activities are designed to reinforce the core approaches of microethnography (describing rather than judging) and praxis (developing theory from practice and developing practice from theory). These video analysis activities are helpful in designing a community viewing experience. Each activity suggestion is provided with the following:

- A suggested level of prior experience in video analysis
- An overview of the activity
- The underlying design components that relate to the particular activity
- An example of the activity with specifics
- A template that can be used to implement the activity
- Optional variations or extensions to the activity

In this way, the activities can be quickly reviewed across the chapters, and those that best fit can be utilized without necessarily using them all or using them in order. This chapter offers four VAT activities:

1. *Lesson de-/reconstruction* → Teachers watch a video of a lesson and try to construct the lesson plan that went with it.
2. *Video-infused lesson study* → Teacher pairs or triads carry out lesson study and then video their delivered lessons, returning to debrief while sharing videos.
3. *Video learning walks* → Video is reviewed in small groups for deeper insights into student learning.
4. *Collaborative inquiry for leaders of teacher learning* → School leaders or teacher educators share their viewpoints from different disciplinary angles.

These activities are intentionally presented with fairly generic teaching behaviors so that they can serve for any grade level or content area and can be readily adapted for use with more specific methods or approaches as a focus.

VAT Activity 1. Lesson De-/Reconstruction

Level of Activity

Introductory, suitable for novice through experienced observers

Overview

Lesson planning is a concrete task that begins in the early stages of learning to teach and continues throughout the span of the teaching career. Research on lesson design has indicated that, while many moments are responsive and "unscripted" in the practice of teaching, well-designed lessons serve two important functions. First, lesson planning supports the design of high-quality practices, tasks, and materials that need to be developed in advance. For instance, differentiating a task by content cannot be done in the moment and requires materials adaptations or the identification of additional resources. Second, lesson plans are windows into teachers' pedagogical reasoning. A teacher's fully developed lesson plan should give a strong indication of their beliefs, knowledge, and professional vision. The alignment between plan and instruction can be yet a further aspect to explore.

Lesson planning is often a challenging skill to master for novices, as it requires a detailed, step-by-step visualization process that depends on prior experience working with learners. By allowing teachers or students of teaching to deconstruct a lesson based on the video of its implementation before asking them to construct it, facilitators can activate teachers' connection-making between the plan and the action. Like the teaching of writing that often begins with deconstruction of a model text before asking learners to construct their own, this activity uses an inductive approach.

This activity could draw on any variety of descriptive, low-inference classroom observation note-taking techniques. It is best begun with a common base video that is associated with a lesson plan and can be then utilized with teacher-created lesson plans and videos from the participant group.

Underlying Design Components

- Because teachers are not asked to observe everything they see but rather capture broad outlines of the activities of the lesson, the observing task becomes more manageable.

- By asking teachers to share and review a common video, viewing norms are established and teachers' follow-up observations can become more reliable and valid.

- By controlling the kinds of notes teachers can make, the possibility of moving into judgment and evaluation is curtailed.

An Example

Step 1. The purpose for the video analysis is set. Participants are told the focus of the VAT activity is to understand how lesson planning relates to instruction.

Step 2. Viewers are asked to watch an entire lesson on video. This video should be no more than 30 minutes and show key lesson elements, such as an opening, teacher modeling, student work, and closure, while certain parts like quiet working period can be edited out. The subject area, grade level, student population, and so forth, can be selected to be relevant to the viewers. (As with all of these activities, the facilitator should try the complete activity first on their own with the video clip they plan to use to ensure it will be workable for the task.) Viewers watch and take descriptive notes along with timestamps, to indicate the different phases of the lesson and what is taking place in each. Often this works well when the viewers have the opportunity to first do this at home so they can stop/play as needed to gather their notes. This VAT task can be practiced using this video, at https://www.youtube.com/watch?v=C8zHoYW2b34&feature=youtu.be, which is of a fourth-grade science lesson, and about thirty minutes long. When using videos retrieved from online sources, make sure to begin the video analysis task after any introductory text or commentary so as not to bias the viewers. Allowing participants to watch "raw" video is essential to all of these tasks. Downloading them from their source enables facilitators to edit them or trim away text and commentary and allows viewing without the labels or comments that might be found next to the video on the host site.

Step 3. Teachers are then asked to compare their "deconstructed" lesson video with a partner. The facilitator can ask teachers to note where they were similar or different. Using their notes, the partners fill in a lesson plan template—one that is locally relevant.

Step 4. The partners then share out to the whole group, and a "master" lesson plan is developed based on the observed teaching. Essentially, viewers are working backward from the lesson itself to discover what the original lesson plan might have contained. If the original lesson plan from the teacher featured in the video is obtainable, that can be an interesting further extension, and participants can compare what the group developed versus the actual lesson plan. Where the teacher deviated, why they might have, and how it impacted the lesson can all be discussed.

Step 5. Teachers then discuss the plan in small groups and determine what they might reconstruct or change in the lesson plan based on what they viewed in its implementation. Pairs come up with possible alternatives.

Step 6. Teachers are given a chance to reflect on the entire VAT activity.

Optional Variations and Extensions

a. Teachers observe for lesson plan design across other subject areas, grade levels, or student populations. Repeated sampling often results in teachers discovering similar patterns as well as important differences.

b. Teachers share lesson plans that they felt went very well and the videos of those lessons where possible.

c. Teachers examine lesson plans that are not clear and create criteria for their design that the community agrees on.

d. Teachers create an ongoing focus for sharing practice around lesson design—for instance, working on lesson closure with their learning community over several sessions.

Template to Guide VAT Activity

Lesson De-/Reconstruction: Focus on Lesson Design

1. Quickwrite: To what extent do you think lesson plans should mirror the actual teaching that happens?

2. Watch the video and use timestamps and descriptions to capture in your notes the lesson phases and activities that you see.

3. Using your observation notes, fill in a lesson plan template that you use in your school. Were there any parts you could not fill in based on the observation of the lesson? What does that signify to you?

4. Share your lesson plan with the group and create a master lesson plan that seems to have been the one this teacher made for this lesson.

5. How might you "reconstruct" or change this lesson plan based on what you viewed in its implementation?

6. Reflect on this video analysis task. What do you think you learned or reinforced from participating in this activity?

VAT Activity 2. Video-Infused Lesson Study

Level of Activity

Intermediate, suitable for observers with some prior experience

Overview

Lesson study, often referred to as Japanese lesson study because of its origins in teacher professional learning in math classrooms in Japan (Chokshi & Fernandez, 2004), is an approach to building teachers' lesson design skills in direct connection with comparing the plan to how the lesson is implemented, by collaborating with others in the planning process, and by viewing others teaching the same lesson. The steps involved in lesson study are generally the following:

1. A group of teachers who are teaching the same lesson work together to create a master lesson plan.

2. Each one teaches the lesson, and the others observe these lessons in turn.

3. The teacher group returns to discuss the lesson as implemented and share observations about how the students were responding.

4. Redesign of the lesson takes place.

What is very effective about lesson study is that it serves as a structure that fosters growth and taps into colleagues as resources for learning. The teachers interact in the planning process, the observation, and the reflection stage through the lens of a particular lesson. This process itself constitutes professional learning that is situated, practice based and knowledge generating (Pella, 2015). According to the Center of Educational Policy Research at Harvard University (2015), "structural separation, in which teachers develop their skills primarily through individual trial and error rather than through observation and collaboration with others, has been a major barrier to improving instruction" (p. 6). Video clearly offers a solution to the barrier of observation. One of the challenges in implementing lesson study is the ability for teachers to have the chance in their daily schedule to observe a colleague teaching the same lesson, but by video recording the lesson under study, teachers can more readily come together later in the week to see the lesson being taught.

Underlying Design Components

- Using a common lesson plan makes the shared viewing especially meaningful to the teacher participants, as each has planned and taught the same lesson so the focus can go directly to the instructional moves.

- Selecting a particular task in the lesson or focusing on a particular student interaction is easier because it is grounded in a lesson plan the participants know.

- Reviewing different approaches across several videos contributes to teachers' appreciation of the richness of the material, as they will discover something new each time.

An Example

Step 1. The purpose for the video analysis is set. Participants are told the focus of the VAT activity is to explore their use of technology in a particular lesson they have recently planned together and individually taught and to bring the lesson plan and a 10-minute video clip of their technology use from that lesson to the session. The teachers are determining the extent to which the technology use supports or hinders student learning in their own teaching as part of this lesson study. They do

(Continued)

(Continued)

a quickwrite about the role they think the technology played in this lesson, based on reflecting on how they had delivered this lesson.

Step 2. Viewers have pre-identified the 10 minutes of their lesson, which features the technology being used. Each teacher brings the clip or has the timestamps for the video, which are all preloaded to a shared site for use on the day of video analysis. If there is time, several clips could be shown in sequence while the whole group watches. Another option is to use several laptops and audio splitters and seat pairs or triads with laptops to simultaneously watch several sets of the 10-minute episodes.

Viewers sit in pairs, watch and take low-inference, descriptive notes, and no discussion is allowed. They are asked to jot down their brief impressions based on that viewing. (As with all of these activities, the facilitator should try the complete activity first on their own with a video clip that may be used to ensure it will be workable for the task.) One that uses technology can be found at https://www.montgomeryschoolsmd.org/departments/development/resources/Alternative_Energy/, from which a ten-minute clip could be selected to illustrate the process. When using videos retrieved from online sources, make sure to begin the video analysis task after any introductory text or commentary so as not to bias the viewers. Allowing participants to watch "raw" video is essential to all of these tasks. Downloading them from their source enables facilitators to edit them or trim away text and commentary and allows viewing without the labels or comments that might be found next to the video on the host site.

Step 3. Teachers discuss the clips in terms of two questions: (1) What evidence of student learning is occurring in this video clip? (2) What part of the learning experience can be directly associated with the technology used?

Step 4. Teachers then see another clip and repeat the process. Teachers should see their own and at least two others.

Step 5. The facilitator invites the group to share their thoughts on how the technology used in this lesson could be enhanced or improved the next time the lesson is taught. The lesson plan is revised.

Step 6. Teachers are given a chance to return to the observation statement they made in Step 1 and reflect on it as well as the entire VAT activity.

Optional Variations and Extensions

a. Teachers do this again together on another clip from another portion of the same lesson, with another focus area.

b. Teachers work just with a partner in the lesson study protocol and exchange and view the whole lesson video to identify areas for discussion and lesson revision.

c. Teachers do this independently with their lesson plan and their lesson video.

Template to Guide VAT Activity

Video Infused Lesson Study: Focus on Technology Use

1. Review the lesson plan and quickwrite: What role do you think this technology played in this lesson?

2. Watch the 10-minute clip of this technology use from your own teaching and that of a colleague. Take low-inference notes.

3. Discuss the clips in terms of two questions: (1) What evidence of student learning is occurring in this video clip? (2) What part of the learning experience can be directly associated with the technology used?

4. Watch the 10-minute clip of this technology use with at least two more colleagues. Take low-inference notes and repeat Step 3.

5. Reflect on this video analysis task. Return to your observation statement in #1 of this template. What do you think of it now? What would you revise or expand in it? What do you think you learned or reinforced from participating in this activity?

VAT Activity 3. Video-Based Learning Walks

Level of Activity

Advanced, suitable for observers with prior experience

Overview

Learning walks (e.g., Downey, Steffy, English, Frase, & Poston, 2004) create opportunities for educators to see classrooms other than their own through structured, quick small-group visits. They are facilitated and utilize protocols that keep participants focused on exploring student learning and avoiding judgment of the teacher.

Sometimes learning walks can be used to help teachers and administrators develop a shared vision as partners, as opposed to engaging in a hierarchical, traditional supervisor-teacher exchange. For instance, a group of teachers, along with coaches and administrators, might spend about 10 minutes in three to four classrooms looking for particular literacy routines that had been introduced at a district-wide professional development session. These visits could also be an opportunity to investigate the ways instruction is taking place on a grade level or across a subject area, with each observer in a team visit capturing different data. One observer might talk with learners; another might note what text and visuals appear in the room; and another observer might note teacher talk. The members of the observing group pool their findings and make sense of patterns and consider implications together. The process reduces teacher isolation and directly informs the shaping of professional vision.

Due to scheduling, which makes it very difficult to set up learning walks, video can be used as a way to "visit" several classrooms. Teachers also do not have to be as anxious about being observed or having the presence of a group of visitors distract their students. By pre-identifying a focus area, teachers can also collect video they are comfortable sharing around a practice they are intentionally implementing. This offers a degree of control over the experience, which may make more teachers willing to try it out. For instance, if there is a school-wide initiative to promote academic language use in all classrooms, teachers can be invited to select a 15-minute clip where observers could find this in action.

Underlying Design Components

- When teachers are asked to focus only on one learner, the observing task becomes more manageable.

- By controlling the kinds of notes teachers can make, the possibility to wander into judgment-making is curtailed and descriptive skills are enhanced.

- When everyone is observing the same video and the facilitator stops to verify findings, there is built-in checking of one's own findings with others.

- Reviewing the video multiple times contributes to teachers' appreciation of the richness of the material, as they will discover something new each time and realize how easy it is to miss interactions in the moment.

An Example

Step 1. The purpose for the video analysis is set. Participants are told the focus of the VAT activity is to explore academic language instruction. The teachers are exploring how academic language instruction is being implemented across the school.

Step 2. Viewers have pre-identified five minutes of their lesson, which features academic language instruction or use. Each teacher brings the clip or has the timestamps for the video, which are all preloaded to a shared site for use on the day of video analysis. The facilitator begins with one video and invites viewers to watch and take low-inference, descriptive notes, and no discussion is allowed. Depending on the size of the group and the nature of the clip, viewers can be assigned to focus on different features as they watch—for instance, to capture the teacher talk, student talk, teacher writing/boardwork, student-to-student talk, and environmental print. They are asked to jot down their brief impressions based on that viewing. (As with all of these activities, the facilitator should try the complete activity first on their own with a video clip that may be used to ensure it will be workable for the task.) A video that shows academic language instruction can be found at https://www.youtube.com/watch?v=w9jRl4rGyr0, from which a three-minute clip could be selected to illustrate the process. When using videos retrieved from online sources, make sure to begin the video analysis task after any introductory text or commentary so as not to bias the viewers. Allowing participants to watch "raw" video is essential to all of these tasks. Downloading them from their source enables facilitators to edit them or trim away text and commentary and allows viewing without the labels or comments that might be found next to the video on the host site.

Step 3. Teachers then share out the observations they made, and the facilitator writes them so all can see. Discussion should follow to link these observations to the development of students' academic language. This discussion should be encouraged, and different conclusions might be drawn based on the evidence. At this point, the group might want the video clip to be played again.

Step 4. Another clip is then shown—for this reason the viewing episodes are only about five minutes, as the intent of the task is to "walk" through several classrooms looking at the same instructional focus rather than going into depth in one lesson.

Step 5. The facilitator invites the group to share their thoughts on what patterns were seen in the instruction of academic language in the classrooms observed and what was not seen. Discussion about how academic language instruction could be enhanced or improved can follow.

Step 6. Teachers are given a chance to reflect on it as well as the entire VAT activity.

Optional Variations and Extensions

a. Teachers can be assigned specific viewing targets so that each member of the viewing team is collecting data on different aspects of the instruction.

b. The activity can be enhanced with the addition of student work products and the lesson plan and other learning materials that were utilized.

c. Video can be selected from various grade levels or subject areas, and the focus can be compared across those settings.

Template to Guide VAT Activity

Video Learning Walks: Focus on Academic Language

1. Quickwrite: Considering the focus of this learning walk is academic language use in our school, what sorts of student and teacher behaviors do you expect to see?

2. Watch the five-minute clip. Take low-inference notes on academic language use—some observers may choose to focus on the teacher's language, their boardwork, a particular student, students' language, and so forth.

3. Discuss the clips in terms of academic language development as seen in this sample.

4. Repeat Steps 2 and 3 several times.

5. Reflect on this video analysis task. What do you think you learned or reinforced from participating in it? What surprised you or stood out to you after looking at this aspect of teaching in the video clip? What did this observation task make you think of changing in your own teaching?

VAT Activity 4. Collaborative Inquiry for Leaders of Teacher Learning

Level of Activity

Advanced, suitable for observers with prior experience

Overview

Participants in this video analysis task are not currently those in elementary or secondary teaching roles but could be coaches, supervisors, administrators, principals in school settings, or teacher education faculty who prepare teachers in higher-education settings. The purpose is to bring those who lead teacher learning together in focused conversation to discuss teaching, anchored in video. Although teachers increasingly have the opportunity to reflect on practice through video analysis, those who lead teacher learning do not often have the opportunity to do so with peers. In particular, expertise building via interchange with colleagues from different disciplinary backgrounds holds great potential at the leadership level, and video is an ideal process to enable this to take place (Baecher & Kung, 2014).

One of the dilemmas faced by those who lead teacher learning is a lack of professional vision for teaching that is outside of their own disciplinary background. For instance, math educators in the role of observing a Spanish lesson or former music teachers carrying out evaluations in special education literacy classrooms may struggle to determine which instructional choices and options are most predictive of student success. Lacking too is a shared taxonomy of and language for a shared professional vision. Grossman and McDonald (2008) state:

> The field of research on teaching still lacks powerful ways of parsing teaching that provide us with the analytic tools to describe, analyze, and improve teaching. Such a framework would help pinpoint both what is common to all examples of teaching, across grade levels and subject areas—such as the ability to engage and motivate learners—and what is more specific to both the subject matter and the context. (p. 185)

This activity pulls together expertise from disparate discipline areas or grade levels in order to explore those common features and to help one another "see" teaching more completely with the addition of other lenses. Even if it occurs once in an academic year, it can be a very powerful learning experience that is then translated into a stronger shared vision and a motivation to hold such sessions for teachers.

Underlying Design Components

- Participants will automatically "see" in new ways as their colleagues bring different lenses, and professional vision will be shaped by those backgrounds.

- The multiplicity of viewpoints can serve to illuminate the complexity of teaching and learning and also create respect and awareness for all that one does not see but others can.

- When everyone is observing the same video and the facilitator stops to verify findings, there is built-in checking of one's own findings with others.

(Continued)

(Continued)

An Example

Step 1. The purpose for the video analysis is set. Participants are told the focus of this VAT activity is to share their expertise for the benefit of all members of the group.

Step 2. A 15-minute video of teaching is carefully selected to align with all of the participants' areas of expertise. For instance, a kindergarten math lesson in which some of the students have learning disabilities and some are English language learners could be shared with a group with backgrounds in early childhood education, mathematics, special education, and teaching English as a second language. (As with all of these activities, the facilitator should try the complete activity first on their own with the video clip they plan to use to ensure it will be workable for the task.) Viewers are asked to first watch the video without taking notes. Any video could be selected from this bank to suit the particular audience members: http://www.doe.mass.edu/edeval/resources/calibration/videos.html, where full-length lesson videos can be found. When using videos retrieved from online sources, make sure to begin the video analysis task after any introductory text or commentary so as not to bias the viewers. Allowing participants to watch "raw" video is essential to all of these tasks. Downloading them from their source enables facilitators to edit them or trim away text and commentary, and allows viewing without the labels or comments that might be found next to the video on the host site.

Step 3. Several questions are posed, which the participants will consider as they review the video through their disciplinary lens. They may choose to watch the video a second time, jot responses to the questions, and then share their perspectives.

Step 4. Teachers are given a chance to reflect on the entire VAT activity.

Optional Variations and Extensions

a. Participants review another clip and try out one another's "lenses."

b. Participants try completing a common evaluation of the lesson with the group and note where they agree or disagree.

c. Participants share perspectives on other artifacts, such as a lesson plan or student work.

d. Participants develop a common set of observation criteria with examples from their disciplines to help in teacher supervision.

Template to Guide VAT Activity

Collaborative Inquiry for Leaders of Teacher Learning: Sharing Expertise

1. Quickwrite: What "lens" do you think you observe teaching through? What kinds of features of instruction do you believe catch your attention based on your teaching background?

2. First, watch the video without taking notes. Then, the second time viewing, consider these questions:

   a. What particular aspects of teaching practice in your discipline were very apparent to you in this clip?

   b. What did you feel you wanted to see but didn't?

   c. What was effective according to "best practices" in your discipline area?

   d. What was questionable according to "best practices" in your discipline area?

3. Reflect on this video analysis task. What do you think you learned or reinforced from participating in it? What surprised you or stood out to you after looking at this aspect of teaching in the student work and in the video clip? What did this observation task make you think of changing in your own teaching?

PUTTING IDEAS INTO ACTION

Looking across the ideas and activities presented in this chapter, consider the following questions:

1. What do you see as common features across all four video analysis activities in this chapter?

2. What skills for video viewing and collaborative conversations might teachers develop if they completed these activities?

3. What teaching skills might teachers develop if they completed these activities?

4. What do you anticipate as problematic, new, or uncomfortable if you were trying these activities out?

5. In what ways could these activities be set up in an online, self-paced format?

6. Which parts of this chapter resonate for you in terms of facilitating other teachers' conversations or for your own use of video analysis?

Chapter References

Baecher, L., & Kung, S. C. (2014). Collaborative video inquiry as teacher educator professional development. *Issues in Teacher Education*, *22*(2), 93–115.

Center for Education Policy Research, Harvard University. (2015). Best foot forward project: Video observation toolkit. *Leveraging Video for Learning*. https://cepr.harvard.edu/publications/best-foot-forward-video-observation-toolkit

Chokshi, S., & Fernandez, C. (2004). Challenges to importing Japanese lesson study: Concerns, misconceptions, and nuances. *Phi Delta Kappan*, *85*(7), 520–525.

Downey, C. J., Steffy, B. E., English, F. W., Frase, L. E., & Poston Jr., W. K. (Eds.). (2004). *The three-minute classroom walk-through: Changing school supervisory practice one teacher at a time*. Thousand Oaks, CA: Corwin.

DuFour, R. (2007). *Leadership strategies for principals (DVD)*. Alexandria, VA: ASCD. http://www.ascd.org/ascd-express/vol5/510-video.aspx

Grossman, P., & McDonald, M. (2008). Back to the future: Directions for research in teaching and teacher education. *American Educational Research Journal*, *45*(1), 184–205.

Pella, S. (2015). Pedagogical reasoning and action: Affordances of practice-based teacher professional development. *Teacher Education Quarterly*, *42*(3), 81–101.

Senge, P. (1990). *The fifth discipline: The art and practice of the learning organization*. New York, NY: Doubleday.

Sherin, M. G., Russ, R. S., Sherin, B. L., & Colestock, A. (2008). Professional vision in action: An exploratory study. *Issues in Teacher Education*, *17*(2), 27–46.

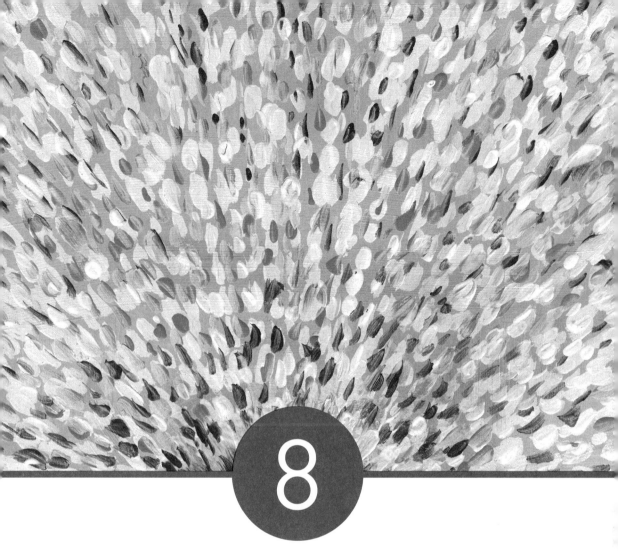

VIDEO USED FOR DEVELOPMENTAL FEEDBACK

One of the greatest moments in anybody's developing experience is when he no longer tries to hide from himself but determines to get acquainted with himself as he really is.

—Norman Vincent Peale, *You Can if You Think You Can* **(1974)**

CHAPTER OBJECTIVES

- To present video analysis of teaching in the context of one-to-one feedback

- To provide a rationale for the effectiveness of video review to support teacher awareness and readiness for change

- To offer coaches and supervisors some considerations for the use of video in their developmental conferences

Chapters 5 through 7 presented approaches for developing teachers' skills in the use of video analysis to support understanding of teaching and learning. The video analysis tasks that were described can be used with any available, relevant video footage or the teachers' own and in small learning groups. In contrast, in this chapter, the focus is exclusively on the use of teachers' own video for the purposes of their individual development, in one-to-one feedback contexts with mentors, coaches, or supervisors. These take place within a teacher education program, such as during student teaching or supervised practicum, or within teacher development carried out in schools with coaches or administrators. In this chapter, four descriptions of approaches to be used in one-to-one formats are presented, each designed to be adapted to address specific pedagogical foci as pertinent to the particular teacher participating. These can be used to introduce teachers to video analysis in ways that still rely on a high degree of structure but could also become less structured depending on the level of the experience of the participants.

DEVELOPMENTAL USES OF VIDEO FOR TEACHER GROWTH

Although analyzing videos of other teachers may be received positively and without resistance, this is quite different from asking teachers to video themselves, watch their video, and discuss specific aspects of their practice with an observer. Because so many teachers have had negative experiences with observation, those must be discussed in an honest way before teachers can fully engage with video analysis.

Indeed, when teachers are asked about their prior experiences with observation and supervision, they often respond emotionally. Many will report feelings of anxiety, trepidation, and insecurity at best and full-on dread and panic at worst. Even when coaches and supervisors do their best to convey that they are there to facilitate the teacher's own goals, to build on their strengths, and to work alongside them on the way—there is always the sense that "teachers, as professionals, can benefit from numerous opportunities to continually refine their craft" (Danielson, 2016). Implicit in "refine their craft" is the growth orientation that can be very positive but also suggests that there is something that the teacher is not yet doing or is not doing well enough, and through the feedback and guidance a coach or supervisor provides, the teacher will be able to improve. Even when coaches or supervisors are being very sensitive to teachers' vulnerabilities in the process of working with them, this is a fundamental and well-documented tension in coaching and supervision (Slick, 1997).

A variety of considerations are suggested as ways to soften the emotional distress of being "supervised" or "coached" and to maximize the potential that the feedback given will be put to good use in the interest of advancing teachers' skills for the benefit of student learning. These include the following:

- Inviting the teacher being observed to self-select the focus for the observation rather than the teacher not knowing what the focus will be.

- Engaging in a pre-observation discussion of the lesson plan so the teacher feels that the coach/supervisor is invested in the success of the lesson rather than having the observation be a "gotcha."

- Observing the class in person at the same time as the video is being recorded, so as to provide the observed teacher data from both sources and to avoid the teacher's perception that the observer missed aspects of the lesson by only seeing the video.

- Ensuring that the video is "owned" by the teacher who has a chance to review it and analyze it prior to the meeting with a coach/supervisor to discuss it.

- Frequently video recording in the classroom to help teachers and students become desensitized to the camera's presence and address the common perception that its presence might distort students' typical behaviors.

- Engaging the coach/supervisor in video recording his/her own practice— either teaching or giving feedback—as a way to heighten their sensitivity to the teachers' experience with the process.

Although not all of these are possible or relevant, depending on the coaching/ supervision context, these are the types of decisions that can be made to support a process that lowers teachers' anxiety as much as possible. These can all work toward shifting the experience toward interactions between teacher and coach/supervisor that feel more supportive than judgmental (Sweeney, 2016).

While there are many types of video analysis activities that could be embedded within coaching/supervision interactions with video, here are four that are appropriate for introducing or continuing to build teachers' professional vision through video analysis work. These activities are designed to reinforce the core approaches of microethnography (describing rather than judging), praxis (developing theory from observing practice and applying theory to understand practice), and cognitive dissonance (generating awareness of the gap between ideal and real). This video analysis is intended to foster individual teacher development. Each activity suggestion is provided with the following:

- A suggested level of prior experience in video analysis

- An overview of the activity

- The underlying design components that relate to the particular activity

- An example of the activity with specifics
- A template that can be used to implement the activity
- Optional variations or extensions to the activity

In this way, the activities can be quickly reviewed across the chapters, and those that best fit can be utilized without necessarily using them all or using them in order. In this chapter, four VAT activities are presented:

1. *Think-aloud playback* → Coaches/supervisors invite teachers to engage in a think-aloud protocol while they watch a replay of a lesson, as a form of dynamic assessment.

2. *Video-enhanced instructional coaching* → Using video to support collaborative coaching conversations about a teacher's growth.

3. *Live-streaming video coaching* → Streaming video is relayed live to a coach who provides on-the-spot suggestions through bug-in-ear technology.

4. *Supervisor/Coach collaborative development* → Those who carry out mentoring or feedback conversations with teachers, video record those conversations and examine their talk with a peer or supervising mentor.

These activities are intentionally presented with fairly generic teaching behaviors so that they can serve for any grade level or content area and can be readily adapted for use with more specific methods or approaches as a focus.

VAT Activity 1. Think-Aloud Playback

Level of Activity

Advanced, suitable for observers with prior experience

Overview

Communicating to teachers that a particular practice is somehow ineffective will naturally put them on the defensive and potentially create resistance to change. However, for teachers to accept and take up feedback, they have to first perceive there is a need to change. Understanding more about resistance (e.g., Hall & Hord, 2015) is important for facilitators of teacher learning, especially with video. One of the most effective aspects of using video is its ability to provide the data that can "establish a need and create a sense of urgency" (Armstrong, 2011, p. 3) and, in turn, illuminate how teachers are thinking. For instance, teachers may genuinely believe that a particular practice is effective and there is no need for change. Therefore, if teachers are questioned about a practice, with their coach/supervisor suggesting they are not implementing it effectively, a problematic conversation can ensue. The coach/supervisor can't really tell if it is the former—that the teacher is being resistant—or the latter—that the teacher really thinks he or she is implementing the practice. Both become frustrated.

However, when a coach/supervisor and a teacher sit together with a video record of practice and coinvestigate a particular instructional practice in the video, the coach/supervisor is able to carry out an on-the-spot, responsive inquiry into the teacher's thinking—a dynamic assessment. Dynamic assessment originates in Vygotsky's (1980) theories of the zone of proximal development and describes the way assessment can happen in an interactive manner. In a dynamic assessment interaction, the educator utilizes probing questions in order to identify an individual's current level of skill and understanding and their proximal level—where they can move with expert assistance.

Golombek (2011) illustrates how a skilled mediator can assist a teacher in arriving at new understandings of their practice when they watch a video playback of the teacher's lesson and the supervisor/coach takes up a dynamic assessment stance rather than an evaluative one. Is the teacher pointing to the practice and do they have a different interpretation of the coach/supervisor's language or vision of this practice? Through the coach/supervisor's probes, the teacher can come to realize that what they thought they were doing is not actually taking place the way they hoped. This opens them up to the possibilities of wanting to learn more about how to achieve the results they seek.

This activity could draw on any variety of classroom observation techniques introduced in Chapter 5, such as event sampling, selective verbatim scripting, and/or coding. It is best begun with a common base video, which allows participants to observe several "cases" of the issue under study, either by providing preselected video clips or by inviting participants to supply their own video clips specifically keyed to the focus of their choosing.

Underlying Design Components

- When teachers are asked to focus only on one learner, the observing task becomes more manageable.

- Using prompts like "notice" and "wonder" keep the task open ended for the teacher to reveal what they are thinking.

- With a specific aspect of teaching to investigate, the conversation between the coach/supervisor and the teacher is focused.

(Continued)

(Continued)

An Example

Step 1. The purpose for the video analysis is set. The teacher opts for/or is told the focus of the VAT activity is to explore differentiated instruction. The teacher captures video of a class in which they have a particular student they wish to focus on. Make sure the camera is positioned to capture this learner clearly, both the visual and the audio. This whole process can be repeated, first with a student who needs more scaffolding and secondly with a student who needs more challenge.

Step 2. The teacher is asked to first watch this video on their own, focusing on the particular student.

Two Noticings/Two Wonderings

What do you

- Notice about the student's behavior?
- Notice about the student's engagement or lesson participation?
- Wonder about your instruction that could be supportive of the student's learning?
- Wonder about your instruction that could be enhanced to support the student's learning?

Step 3. The teacher then shares their video with their coach/supervisor using a secure, online platform. The coach/supervisor also reviews the video with these open-ended questions in mind. They then set a time to meet to discuss the lesson, where they can also watch portions of the video on a shared computer.

Step 4. Watch portions of the video together, first portions (three to six minutes in length) that the teacher selects, and then portions that the coach/supervisor suggests watching. The coach/supervisor asks these same four questions (Two Noticings/Two Wonderings), and the teacher shares his or her observations and reflections. The coach/supervisor's role is to try to better understand the teacher's thinking through the observations and reflections they share.

Step 5. Teachers are given a chance to return to reflect on the entire VAT activity with differentiated instruction as a focus.

Optional Variations and Extensions

a. Teachers and coaches/supervisors could watch the video for the first time together, if there is not enough time for them to preview it separately beforehand.

b. Specific criteria for differentiated instruction could be prepared and used as a reference for the viewing.

c. Teachers and coach/supervisors first do this task on a video found online, not the teacher's own, to establish the process.

d. Other categories of instruction or other student populations could be selected as a focus. The same process could be carried out twice, first with a student who needs more scaffolding and secondly with a student who needs more challenge. Steps to take in subsequent lesson plans would be discussed to further assess the teacher's reflection-for-action.

Template to Guide VAT Activity

Think-Aloud Playback: Focus on Differentiation

1. Capture video of a class in which you have a particular student who needs additional supports (or who accelerates through the materials) in the class. Make sure the camera is positioned to capture this learner clearly, both the visual and the audio.

2. Watch this video first on your own, focusing on the particular student.

   Two Noticings/Two Wonderings

   What do you

   • Notice about the student's behavior?

   • Notice about the student's engagement or lesson participation?

   • Wonder about your instruction that could be supportive of the student's learning?

   • Wonder about your instruction that could be enhanced to support the student's learning?

3. Share your video with your coach/supervisor. The coach/supervisor also reviews the video with these open-ended questions in mind. Set a time to meet to discuss the lesson.

4. Watch portions of the video together, first portions (three to six minutes in length) that the teacher selects and then portions that the coach/supervisor suggests watching. The coach/supervisor asks these same four questions (Two Noticings/Two Wonderings), and the teacher shares his or her observations and reflections.

5. Reflect on this video analysis task. What do you think you learned or reinforced about differentiation from participating in it?

VAT Activity 2. Video-Enhanced Instructional Coaching

Level of Activity

Advanced, suitable for more experienced observers

Overview

Participating in coaching/ongoing supervision usually involves a recurring cycle, which involves the teacher and coach/supervisor in looking at teaching improvement goals, planning, delivering instruction, and reflecting on planning, instruction, and student work, with an eye to meeting those goals and then setting new ones. What is so powerful about introducing video into the coaching cycle is the possibility for teachers to get a chance to see their own practice and work in greater synchronicity with the coaches that are invested in their growth. Knight (2014) provides a variety of possible directions to take when choosing to infuse video into instructional coaching, which may occur between a school leader and a teacher, peer teachers, or other combinations, but are all enriched by the addition of video artifacts.

Unleashing the Potential of Video in Coaching/Supervision

In successful teacher coaching/supervision, there are a variety of necessary elements—many of which are social/emotional/psychological. On the teacher's side, they relate to their readiness, willingness, and sense of a need to change. On the supervisor's side, they have to do with the coach/supervisor's skills at noticing what is important to notice, being selective around which high-leverage practices to focus on, and providing feedback in ways that the teacher will listen to and accept without shutting down. Video can be instrumental in bringing the teacher and coach/supervisor together to build a shared vision, grounded in the evidence that can be seen and discussed in video review. This is true both because of the chance for the coach/supervisor to assess teacher thinking as they watch the lesson together via video and because of the cognitive dissonance the teacher may experience as he or she sees that what they thought was taking place is not what is actually taking place.

Cognitive dissonance is a psychological state of unease and disequilibrium that results from recognizing a disconnect between what we perceive to be true and what has actually occurred or between an image we held of ourselves and evidence that challenges that image. It could be as simple as hearing our own voices on an audiotape, which is often jarring and bizarre, or as complicated as watching ourselves teach and realizing that what we thought was taking place at the time is not what we are witnessing on the video playback. Fuller and Manning (1973) emphasized the sense of vulnerability and real distress that "confronting" oneself on video can cause, while also suggesting that this creates a powerful opening for honest conversations and individuals setting out to change behaviors they are displeased to see.

Dissonance between perception and evidence can foster teachers' beliefs that there is a need to change and is the core psychological rationale for the effectiveness of video analysis in skill development.

In concert with video analysis, the Johari Window (Luft & Ingham, 1961) is a helpful conceptual framework that reminds both coaches and teachers about the way both self-disclosure and feedback can operate to open up new understandings. What is unique about the Johari Window is that it sheds light not just on what the teacher sees or does not see but also on what the observer (coach/supervisor) sees or does not see—for the process of coaching is

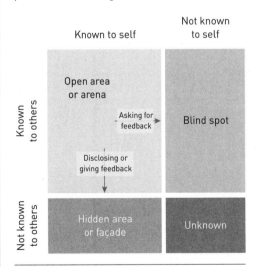

Source: Adapted from Luft, J. and Ingham, H. (1955). "The Johari window, a graphic model of interpersonal awareness". *Proceedings of the western training laboratory in group development*. Los Angeles: University of California, Los Angeles.

as much about the coach's learning as the teacher's. The Johari Window can be used as a visual representation of four dimensions of "seeing," two from the point of view of the teacher and two from the coach's/supervisor's. The first arena is what both the teacher and the coach/supervisor can "see" and recognize as the teacher's strengths and areas for growth. The second arena is the "blind" spot for the teacher, where the coach can see what the teacher cannot yet see. As mentioned earlier, the coach/supervisor can better understand what this teacher thinking is through dynamic assessment as they watch a video of teaching and unpack what they are seeing, often leading to the teacher's sense of cognitive dissonance. The goal of instructional coaching/supervision is to shrink this area. The third area represents what the teacher hides from the coach/supervisor out of fear or embarrassment, which can only be shared when trust is built between them. Finally, the fourth area is the terrain that is yet unconsidered or unknown to both the teacher and the coach/supervisor. Its presence is only realized in hindsight or through shared understandings made jointly—which collaborative video is uniquely suited to reveal.

Underlying Design Components

- With a specific aspect of teaching to investigate, the conversation between the coach/supervisor and the teacher is focused.

- Because teachers are not asked to take open-ended notes on a variety of aspects of their practice but rather to just tally questions and responders, the observing task becomes more manageable.

- Since teachers are asked to tally a concrete observable, as opposed to something like "look for higher order thinking," it makes the viewing more reliable.

An Example

Step 1. The purpose for the video analysis is set by both the teacher and the coach/supervisor. This focus might be related to a personal goal or a school or district-wide initiative. In this example, the focus is the way the teacher calls on students or chooses responders, after the teacher and coach note that the same few students seem to be answering all the teacher's questions. How teachers distribute response opportunities indicate how they are engaging all learners in the classroom and informally gauging student understanding.

Step 2. The teacher and coach choose a routine day for video recording. The coach/supervisor could be present or not, and a complete lesson is recorded. The teacher then watches the lesson using a tallying form to note response opportunities, as in the provided guide.

Step 3. The teacher and coach then set up a time to meet and review eight minutes or so of the lesson together. The teacher could choose which portion to watch, or the coach/supervisor might do so. This is where teachers who are in arena 2 of the Johari Window will seek to hide what they perceive to be unfavorable from the supervisor/coach's view.

Step 4. Using the data the teacher has collected and what the teacher and coach/supervisor might jointly collect during their shared viewing, they describe what they are finding. This hopefully moves the conversation into arena 2 and 4, so that both teacher and coach/supervisor are making discoveries.

Step 5. The teacher and coach/supervisor are given a chance to reflect on the entire VAT activity as well as to set new goals for growth.

Optional Variations and Extensions

a. Teachers and coach/supervisors could watch the video for the first time together, if there isn't time for them to preview it separately beforehand.

b. The same process could be carried out several times, until the teacher and coach/supervisor feel that improvement has been made.

c. Teachers and coach/supervisors first do this task on a video available online, not the teacher's own, to establish the process.

d. Other categories of instruction could be selected as a focus.

e. Teachers carry this process out in the role of peer instructional coaches. For more information on this process, see https://www.wested.org/resources/cftl-centerview-video-based-peer-coaching/.

Template to Guide VAT Activity

Video Enhanced Instructional Coaching: Focus on Response Opportunities

1. Meet with your coach/supervisor to set a target for the video-based instructional coaching cycle.

2. Video a lesson and upload it so your coach/supervisor can access it.

3. Using the provided tally sheet, watch about 20 minutes of your video in which there are a lot of questions posed to students. Mark the responders to your questions.

4. Review about eight minutes of your lesson with your supervisor/coach, in which there were many questions posed. What discoveries do the two of you make when watching this segment and using the viewing tally sheet?

5. Reflect on this video analysis task. What do you think you learned or reinforced from participating in it?

Observation Guide: Response Opportunities

To investigate this aspect of teaching and learning, view 20 minutes of your video clip where there is teacher-whole class interaction and, using the instrument below, note all the questions you see yourself posing. Then, using the checklist, determine in each instance of a question being posed to the class, which students are responding.

Student Responder						
Note all questions teacher poses here:	Male?	Female?	Sitting close to teacher?	Sitting far from teacher?	Whole-class, choral (calling out) response?	Whole-class, partner talk?
1.						
2.						
3.						

1. What surprised you or stood out to you after looking at this aspect of teaching in the video clip?

2. What did this observation task make you think of changing in your own teaching?

3. What specific alternatives do you now see could have occurred that might have increased response opportunities in this lesson?

VAT Activity 3. Live-Streaming Video Coaching

Level of Activity

Advanced, suitable for teachers who have some experience with traditional observation

Overview

Often, coaching/supervision involves delayed feedback, provided hours, days, or even weeks after an observation. In contrast, immediate feedback—delivered close in time to the observed teaching—has been shown to be a potentially very effective practice. In a review of the literature, Scheeler, Ruhl, and McAfee (2004) found that immediate feedback resulted in faster and more efficient acquisition of teachers' learning targets than delayed feedback. However, it is not easy to interrupt a lesson or walk over to provide teachers feedback while they are being observed, since that would obviously be disruptive to them and their learners and could be perceived as undermining their authority. In addition, it can be difficult to schedule feedback sessions immediately after an observed lesson with overloaded coach/supervisor schedules. A relatively new solution has been the use of live-streaming video coaching in combination with "bug-in-ear" technology. This works via Skype or another live streaming video platform. Remotely, a coach watches the lesson live and keeps the "line" open while the observed teacher wears a wireless, Bluetooth earphone to be able to hear what the coach says in a discrete way that would appear seamless to the students in the room.

The process of providing bug-in-ear coaching has been advanced by Rock (e.g., Rock, Zigmond, Gregg, & Gable, 2011). She describes the feedback as specific, descriptive, and consisting of mostly praise with some precise suggestions. The possibility for the coach to redirect a lesson and offer on-the-spot feedback to support the teacher is the central feature of live-streamed coaching. Rock also recommends limiting the feedback delivered in this way to no more than 30 minutes and following it up with one-to-one coaching conversations after the fact. Although daunting at first, she has found that after a little practice, most teachers are able to adjust to the complexity of delivering their lesson while still being able to attend to the coach's commentary.

Underlying Design Components

- In this model, coaches enter the teaching in a way that shifts their role from unobtrusive observer, and this has the potential to more fully engage the teacher in the feedback experience.

- While the video is being live streamed, it gives the coach the opportunity to see the lesson from a different perspective than being there in person; the coach may possibly be able to notice and prevent problems from arising or continuing.

- By providing the teacher the opportunity to react and change direction in the delivery of the lesson rather than after the fact, trust and collaboration can be enhanced with the coach.

An Example

Step 1. The purpose for the video analysis is set. Teachers are told the focus of this VAT activity is to explore classroom management, linking the target of observation to student learning. For instance, providing a positive framework for classroom interaction will promote student engagement.

Step 2. Teachers start out in a "staged" session for practice. The teacher wears a wireless earpiece connected to a video call (such as Skype, Google Hangouts, or Zoom) or to a cell phone call, with the observer in the room. The teacher begins a "lesson" and becomes accustomed to listening to the input from the observer while still carrying on with his or her lesson. It is highly recommended

(Continued)

(Continued)

to practice this in low-stakes settings a few times—such as with colleagues, in an after-school setting, or with small-group instruction—before carrying it out in a full lesson.

Step 3. The observer and the teacher review some of the categories for classroom management, as in the provided guide, so that they share a common language for the kinds of behaviors and events that they will be noticing for this technology-enhanced live coaching experience. Not all of these would be commented on during the observation, but some might be particularly relevant.

Step 4. During a live lesson, the observer provides commentary to the teacher focused on their classroom management. For every four positive comments, it is recommended that one suggestion is made (https://gtlcenter.org/sites/default/files/Bug-in-ear_Coaching.pdf). The observer also logs a running record of the comments they are making.

Step 5. After the lesson, the teacher and observer discuss the lesson through the classroom management lens. They may go back to the video and discuss moments when the observer provided a comment (praise or redirection) and consider the teacher's reflection *in* action versus reflection *on* action (Schön, 1987).

Optional Variations and Extensions

a. Teachers and observers watch a video lesson from the teacher and review the observation targets together prior to engaging in the bug-in-ear live feedback process.

b. After using bug-in-ear coaching for one aspect of practice, such as classroom management, they then move on to look at other relevant practice areas.

c. Teachers use video conferencing tools to receive live coaching on their planning or assessment practices, engaging with their coach/supervisor to think aloud through those activities.

Template to Guide VAT Activity

Technology-Enhanced Live Coaching: Focus on Classroom Management

1. Think about what effective classroom management entails for you. Jot down your ideas here.

2. Use the provided video viewing guide for aspects of classroom management and review those with your coach/supervisor. Make sure that the language is jargon-free and you can really understand what these aspects "look like" in practice.

3. Set up Skype/video conferencing and the wireless headset and practice with the coach/supervisor in the room and remotely. Try out a small session of 15 minutes with a small group.

4. Carry out a full lesson and engage with live-streaming video coaching. Also have the coach video record the session.

5. Reflect on this video analysis task. What do you think you learned or reinforced from participating in it? What surprised you or stood out to you after looking at this aspect of teaching in the video clip? What did this observation task make you think of changing in your own teaching?

Observation Guide: Classroom Management

Review these aspects of classroom management to explore your understanding of how these "look" during a lesson observation.

How does the teacher . . .

-   Arrange the room to optimize the particular activities being implemented?
-   Display the classroom rules as well as rights, expectations, and responsibilities?
-   Remind students of classroom routines and procedures?
-   Incentivize students to stay on task?
-   Use verbal and nonverbal/physical movement cues to stay on task?
-   Give instructions to students?
-   Manage materials distribution?
-   Manage lesson pacing/time on each lesson component?
-   Praise or encourage positive student behavior?
-   Talk with students, and how do students talk with each other?
-   Respond to disruptive behavior?
-   Promote positive relationships with and among students?
-   Develop students' social skills?
-   Support students' problem-solving or decision-making skills?

Source: Adapted from Planning *Classroom Management*, 2nd edition, by Karen Bosch. Thousand Oaks, CA: Corwin Press, www.corwinpress.com.

VAT Activity 4. Supervisor/Coach Collaborative Development

Level of Activity

Advanced, suitable for experienced observers

Overview

The feedback provided to teachers by their supervisors, in preservice and in-service settings, is considered to be essential to teacher learning. As we have seen in this chapter, incorporating video records into these mentoring sessions has been shown to trigger the cognitive dissonance needed to help teachers explore the gaps between their intentions and their actual behaviors. However, although we ask teachers to examine their teaching practice via video, their coaches/supervisors are not engaging in a parallel examination of their supervisory/coaching practice. For the most part, supervisors and coaches who carry out these critical conversations with teachers do so without feedback about how they are performing in those conferences, and rarely do they receive opportunities for their own growth.

Researchers have discussed how complex the work of coaching/supervising is and, during the feedback conversation, have identified skills exhibited by coaches/supervisors such as the following: noticing, pointing, ignoring, intervening, unpacking, and processing (Burns & Badiali, 2016). However, rather than facilitating teachers doing this instructional analysis and in spite of their best intentions, supervisors/coaches tend to dominate feedback session talk, telling rather than asking, and generally do the work of noticing, unpacking, and processing *for* the teacher (Farr, 2010). Improving the quality of these feedback sessions depends on coaches/supervisors becoming more aware of these conversational tendencies in general and in particular their own behaviors during conference talk. Thus, professional learning that could target coach/supervisor awareness of their talk in post-observation feedback sessions is clearly relevant.

Although supervisors/coaches may be familiar with supporting teachers' looking at their videos of classroom lessons, they are often unfamiliar with looking at their mentoring conversations on video. Supervisors/coaches may feel even more vulnerable than teachers do, since they consider themselves or believe they should be seen as "experts." For these reasons, it is essential to allow supervisors/coaches to first watch video of mentoring conversations of unknown other dyads to determine some of the criteria they believe is important and then look at their own videos of feedback conversations privately, without an expectation that they will publicly share their videos. Once they are ready, viewing a feedback session with a trusted coach/supervisor colleague can be greatly beneficial for growth (Baecher & Beaumont, 2017).

Underlying Design Components

- The design of this activity is focused on self-development in combination with supportive peer interaction, to minimize loss of face and resistance among supervisor/coach participants.

- By using a structured viewing guide for supervisors/coaches to examine their feedback conversations with teachers, the process of looking at their own and others' videos becomes more objective.

- Sharing just their findings or the videos themselves is a powerful self- and peer-development experience for supervisors/coaches who are often not beneficiaries themselves of the feedback process they provide to others.

An Example

Step 1. The purpose for the video analysis is set. Coaches/supervisors are told the focus of this VAT activity is to explore their feedback sessions with teachers, linking the target of observation to teacher learning. Making connections between their talk and the teachers' talk is challenging to do in the moment, and video provides them the unusual opportunity to reflect on their coaching/supervisory practice.

Step 2. Supervisors/coaches are shown a video of a supervisor/coach in a post-observation conversation. (As with all of these activities, the facilitator should try the complete activity first on their own with the video clip they plan to use to ensure it will be workable for the task.) Viewers watch about 10 minutes of the video and complete notes in the provided structured viewing guide. This could look like the one provided after the template below. This VAT task can be practiced using this video, at https://eleducation.org/resources/coaching-for-change-giving-feedback, which is about three minutes long. When using videos retrieved from online sources, make sure to begin the video analysis task after any introductory text or commentary so as not to bias the viewers. Allowing participants to watch "raw" video is essential to all of these tasks. Downloading them from their source enables facilitators to edit them or trim away text and commentary, and allows viewing without the labels or comments that might be found next to the video on the host site.

Step 3. Supervisors/coaches then share their findings from their viewing guides with a partner, and then the facilitator leads a whole group discussion about their noticings in the categories of the viewing guide. The facilitator will have to ensure that the observations stay descriptive and do not become evaluations of the coaching/supervision as a whole.

Step 4. Supervisors/coaches can have time to video one of their own feedback sessions, with permission of the teacher, and then examine it using the same viewing guide. Their self-reflections can then be shared with peers, or peers can then watch each other's videos and then meet to discuss what they found.

Optional Variations and Extensions

a. The facilitator can begin by video recording and analyzing one of their own feedback conversations and use that to begin the process. This shows the other supervisors/coaches that we can all learn from viewing and analyzing our practice.

b. The activity can be run completely online, with the videos and the observation guides being completed via the web, and then live, synchronous conversations can take place.

c. Supervisors/coaches can share these videos with the teachers in the video-recorded feedback sessions and invite them to provide their insights and reflections on the feedback conversations and how they see themselves interacting in these conversations.

Template to Guide VAT Activity

Supervisor/Coach Collaborative Development: Focus on Feedback Conversations

1. Watch the video of a supervisor/coach and a teacher in a feedback session, and without talking to anyone, write down your observations of the talk using the provided viewing guide.

2. Share your findings with a partner and then the group of other coaches/supervisors. What did you notice and wonder about when examining a feedback conversation about the supervisor's/coach's talk and the teacher's talk?

3. Video a feedback session with a teacher you are supervising/coaching and examine it using the same viewing guide. Bring just the findings, or exchange your video with a peer coach/supervisor. Come back together to discuss what you noticed/learned when you tried this out on your own coaching/supervisory practice.

4. Reflect on this video analysis task. What do you think you learned or reinforced from participating in it? What surprised you or stood out to you after looking at this aspect of teaching in the video clip? What did this observation task make you think of changing in your own teaching?

Video Viewing Guide: Analyzing Post-Observation Conference Talk

Your Name (Supervisor/Coach):

Teacher's Name:

Features		Video Analysis
What was the nature of the teacher's talk?	Your general impressions	
	Questions you heard the teacher asking	
	Discoveries you saw the teacher making	
What was the nature of the supervisor's/coach's talk?	Questions you heard the supervisor/coach asking	

Features	Video Analysis
Suggestions you heard the supervisor/coach making	
Supervisor's/coach's use of praise	
What were the phases of the conversation the supervisor/coach seemed to move through?	
Was there use of the lesson plan?	
Was there use of student work?	
Body language and nonverbal signals from supervisor/coach or teacher?	
Your • Take-aways • Learning • Noticings • Wonderings from doing this analysis	

PUTTING IDEAS INTO ACTION

Looking across the ideas and activities presented in this chapter, consider the following questions:

1. What do you see as common features across all four video analysis activities in this chapter?

2. What skills for video viewing might teachers/coaches/supervisors develop if they completed these activities?

3. What do you anticipate as problematic, new, or uncomfortable if you were trying these activities out with participants?

4. In what ways could these activities be set up in an online, self-paced format?

5. Which parts of this chapter resonate for you in terms of facilitating other educators' conversations or for your own use of video analysis?

Chapter References

Armstrong, A. (2011). Key strategies help educators overcome resistance to change. *The Professional Learning Association-Learning Forward*, *14*(2), 1–7.

Baecher, L., & Beaumont, J. (2017). Supervisor reflection for teacher education: Video-based inquiry as model. *The European Journal of Applied Linguistics*, *6*(2), 65–84.

Burns, R. W., & Badiali, B. (2016). Unearthing the complexities of clinical pedagogy in supervision: Identifying the pedagogical skills of supervisors. *Action in Teacher Education*, *38*(2), 156–174.

Danielson, C. (2016). Charlotte Danielson on rethinking teacher evaluation. *Education Week*, *35*(28), 20, 24. https://www.edweek.org/ew/articles/2016/04/20/charlotte-danielson-on-rethinking-teacher-evaluation.html

Farr, F. (2010). *The discourse of teaching practice feedback: A corpus-based investigation of spoken and written modes* (Vol. 12). New York, NY: Routledge.

Fuller, F. F., & Manning, B. A. (1973). Self-confrontation reviewed: A conceptualization for video playback in teacher education. *Review of Educational Research*, *43*(4), 469–528.

Golombek, P. R. (2011). Dynamic assessment in teacher education: Using dialogic video protocols to intervene in teacher thinking and activity. In K. E. Johnson & P. R. Golombek, (Eds.), *Research on second language teacher education: A sociocultural perspective on professional development* (pp. 121–135). New York, NY: Routledge.

Hall, G. E., & Hord, S. M. (2015). *Implementing change: Patterns, principles, and potholes*. 4th Ed. Boston, MA: Pearson.

Knight, J. (2014). *Focus on teaching: Using video for high-impact teaching*. Thousand Oaks, CA: Corwin.

Luft, J., & Ingham, H. (1961). The Johari Window: A graphic model of awareness in interpersonal relations. *Human Relations Training News*, *5*(9), 6–7.

Rock, M. L., Zigmond, N. P., Gregg, M., & Gable, R. A. (2011). The power of virtual coaching. *Educational Leadership*, *69*(2), 4–48.

Scheeler, M. C., Ruhl, K. L., & McAfee, J. K. (2004). Providing performance feedback to teachers: A review. *Teacher Education and Special Education*, *27*(4), 396–407.

Schön, D. A. (1987). *Educating the reflective practitioner: Toward a new design for teaching and learning in the professions*. San Francisco, CA: Jossey-Bass.

Slick, S. (1997). Assessing versus assisting: The supervisor's roles in the complex dynamics of the student teaching triad. *Teaching and Teacher Education*, *13*(7), 713–726.

Sweeney, D. (2016). *How can we avoid coaching that feels evaluative?* Retrieved from https://dianesweeney.com/how-can-we-avoid-coaching-that-feels-evaluative/

Vygotsky, L. S. (1980). *Mind in society: The development of higher psychological processes*. Boston, MA: Harvard University Press.

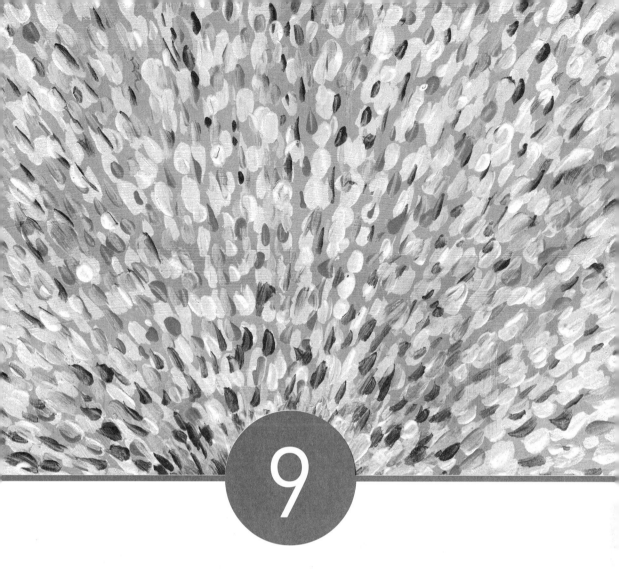

9

VIDEO USED FOR
EVALUATIVE FEEDBACK

Evaluate what you want—because what gets measured,
gets produced.

—James Belasco

CHAPTER OBJECTIVES

- To present video analysis of teaching in the context of teacher performance assessment

- To emphasize the effectiveness of video review to support consistency, validity, and utility in teacher evaluation

- To offer coaches and supervisors possibilities for using video in their evaluations of teacher performance

Chapters 5 through 7 presented approaches for developing teachers' skills in the use of video analysis to support understanding of teaching and learning, while Chapter 8 turned to the role of observation and feedback in conjunction with video to support teacher development. In continuation, this chapter focuses on the ways video can be used to support evaluation efforts that are implemented to assess, monitor, and improve teaching. These can take place within a teacher education program, such as during student teaching or supervised practicum, or within professional development and evaluation systems carried out in schools with coaches or administrators. In this chapter, four descriptions of evaluative approaches are presented, each designed to be adapted to address specific pedagogical foci as pertinent to the particular evaluation contexts.

EVALUATIVE USES OF VIDEO FOR TEACHER GROWTH

Chapter 8 stressed the importance of great sensitivity toward teachers being asked to share their videos for the purposes of gaining developmental feedback. The sense of vulnerability that sharing one's teaching on video provokes is clearly heightened when one considers adding in evaluation to the mix. In Chapter 8, the use of video to provide clarity around lesson events, the chance for teachers to self-reflect, and the ways video can be utilized for dynamic assessment in the coaching interaction process were all key to its application in a developmental approach.

Yet, at times there is a need for performance-based evaluation of teaching. Evaluation provides teachers and those who work with teachers a ranking of performance relative to set criteria, in relation to others, and in terms of individual improvement targets. It is ideally accompanied by a developmental process that builds on teachers' strengths and supports areas needing improvement. Although evaluation connotes judgment, punitive measures, and anxiety, it can also be a source of recognition, achievement, and success. Evaluations of teaching are certainly unavoidable, and they are a critical component of district-level teacher evaluation systems and as part of certification coursework in teacher education. However, the use of video in teacher evaluation, in addition to traditional in-person classroom observations, is a relatively new development. Using findings from large-scale trials through the *Measures of Effective Teaching* (MET) study (http://k12education .gatesfoundation.org/blog/measures-of-effective-teaching-met-project/) has greatly contributed to understanding more about its use.

One study used MET data to address concerns that administrators had about using videos that teachers had selected to share for evaluation. They wondered whether teachers were going to submit "best foot forward" samples that would not be representative. To test this theory, teachers were asked, from a set of videos of their lessons that had been recorded, to choose which lesson videos they wished to submit for their evaluations. Both the teacher-selected videos and those they had not selected were submitted for scoring, with the raters unaware of which type they were evaluating. The study concluded that

> the rankings of teaching practice on teacher-chosen videos were similar to rankings one would have had on a broader sample of a teacher's videos. . . . While most teachers performed better on the selected videos (a good sign, since it implies that teachers understood which of their lessons would score better on their rubric), the rankings were largely the same on the teacher-selected lessons as on the non-selected lessons (Kane, Gehlbach, Greenburg, Quinn, & Thal, 2015, pp. 9–10).

This study and other studies conducted by the *Best Foot Forward* project at Harvard University have shown that video records can be reliably used to measure teacher quality, even when teachers choose which clips to share. They outline key findings, based on their research with principals and teachers on using video for teacher evaluation.

Key Findings From Experimental Research on Video in Teacher Evaluation	Teachers are willing to record and watch their lessons when they have control over the camera and can select the videos they wish to submit for evaluation purposes. Both administrators and teachers strongly agreed that they would continue with the use of video in teacher evaluation in the future.
	Using video resulted in teachers lowering their self-assessment ratings and led to their realization that there was much that was going on that they had not previously been aware of.
	Post-observation conversations shifted, with teachers perceiving greater fairness and specificity in the feedback they received from administrators, and administrators found teachers less defensive.
	About 85% of administrators reported that the video-based observations freed up substantial time for them during the school day, and they were able to shift the observation and rating process to quieter times.
	Allowing teachers to choose which videos to submit for evaluation did not affect administrators' ability to note weaker teaching performance, as the submitted videos correlated with live-observation findings.

One of the best ways to maximize the potential of video in teacher evaluation is to simply do both—carry out in-person evaluation as traditionally done and add in video-based evaluation. It can be helpful to look at them side by side.

10 FEATURES OF IN-PERSON AND VIDEO-BASED OBSERVATION FOR TEACHER EVALUATION

	Traditional In-Person Observation in Teacher Evaluation	Video-Based Observation in Teacher Evaluation
1	Visitor in the evaluation role captures observation information.	The camera captures observational data.
2	Visitor takes notes, which constitute the data for analysis.	The video record constitutes the data for analysis.
3	The observed lesson may or may not be one the teacher wishes to have observed.	The observed lesson is the one the teacher wishes to have observed.
4	The observer must stay for the duration of the period to capture data on the entirety of the lesson.	The observer may leave early and still be able to watch the remainder of the lesson at a later time.
5	The visitor may or may not have the disciplinary expertise of the observed teacher.	Using distance observation can "bring in" observers with the disciplinary expertise of the observed teacher.
6	Calibration of scoring for the observed lesson cannot take place unless multiple viewers visit the same class at the same time.	Calibration of scoring for the observed lesson can take place as multiple viewers can assess the same lesson simultaneously or over a period of time.
7	The observer is the one with the authority, memory, and data to assess the lesson.	The observed teacher and the observer can both assess the lesson.
8	When completing a performance rubric, observers rely on memory for aspects of the lesson where there is no recorded data.	When completing a performance rubric, observers can review the video record.
9	During the post-observation conference, where teacher and observer have perceptual differences the observer's notes are used.	During the post-observation conference, the video can be consulted where teacher and observer have perceptual differences.
10	To look at teacher growth, notes over several observation visits can be reviewed.	To look at teacher growth, video clips over time can be reviewed.

These ten features of video-based observation clearly indicate how the addition of video is beneficial to the evaluation process. In Chapter 8, many of these benefits were also conferred on the coaching/developmental feedback process. In this chapter, four approaches to incorporating video-based evaluation are presented but, in general, are closely related to developmental approaches. Each approach is provided with

- A suggested level of prior experience in video analysis
- An overview of the activity
- The underlying design components that relate to the particular activity
- An example of the activity with specifics
- A template that can be used to implement the activity
- Optional variations or extensions to the activity

In this way, the activities can be quickly reviewed across the chapters, and those that best fit can be utilized without necessarily using them all or using them in order. In this chapter, four VAT activities are presented:

1. *Calibration of observers* → The use of video to support inter-rater reliability among a number of observers.

2. *Self-assessment via video* → Teachers are trained on the use of a viewing rubric and then apply that rubric to evaluate their own practice.

3. *Distance supervision* → Teachers submit video to coaches/supervisors who are situated remotely and provide evaluative feedback.

4. *Video in teacher portfolios* → Teachers submit video and video analysis to supervisors who then score the lesson and the reflection as part of a formal teacher evaluation system.

These activities are intentionally presented with fairly generic teaching behaviors, so that they can serve for any grade level or content area and can be readily adapted for use with more specific methods or approaches as a focus.

VAT Activity 1. Calibration of Observers

Level of Activity

Advanced, suitable for experienced observers

Overview

If the purpose of teacher evaluation is to improve teaching practice, then the most important place to start when implementing a teacher evaluation process is to ensure that the observers have jointly participated in calibration exercises. Through calibration activities, the observed (teachers) and the observer (instructional coaches, school administrators, and district leaders) are given the opportunity to learn to observe samples of teaching in local contexts carefully and descriptively. Too often, there is implementation of rubrics, checklists, or other evaluation instruments based on a false assumption that all participants already possess a shared professional vision. Video is an essential tool for use in calibration work, and because high-quality calibration training is so important for teachers' ability to self-assess as well as to be evaluated by administrators, additional attention to this component of teacher evaluation is provided here.

First, a few principles to consider as calibration exercises are being designed include the following:

1. Teacher evaluation depends on human judgment, which in turn is inherently biased. Forms of bias that all observers tap into, both conscious and subconscious, must be brought out for discussion to increase the likelihood that the observer will attempt to reduce their occurrence. For instance, when evaluators know they will have to discuss their ratings face-to-face with teachers, they are much more likely to inflate their scores (Graham, Milanowski, & Miller, 2012). In addition, prior experiences with a teacher will influence the evaluation (either in a positive direction, as in Halo effect, or in a negative way). Also, teachers of high-performing pupils also tend to be scored higher than those who teach low-performing ones (Whitehurst, Chingos, & Lindquist, 2014).

2. Inter-rater agreement is the goal of calibration activities. That is, not that raters rate reliably but that they concur reliably on the exact scores. Because most teacher evaluation systems have only three or four levels of performance—from ineffective to effective—or even two levels (satisfactory/unsatisfactory), evaluators should be able to agree on the exact same score when making evaluations.

3. Observers will fall into three categories: those who are able to consistently identify evidence that corresponds to the rating system; those who are somewhat able to do so but need to improve in certain areas; and those who struggle to identify meaningful evidence of effective instruction. All observers can improve their ability to "see" if they have ongoing opportunities to develop their observation skills and understanding of the vision of effective teaching captured in the evaluation instruments they must employ.

4. All observers need routine "re-calibration" events to ensure that they are consistent and fair in their scoring practices. These should occur both individually and in group sessions. These should be granular enough to determine in which areas inter-rater agreement is more problematic, so these can be specifically addressed.

Underlying Design Components

- Because observers are not asked to rate everything they see because of the restriction of focusing only on one aspect of classroom practice or one learner at a time, the observing task becomes more manageable.

- Supporting the use of description before evaluation (D comes before E) enables observers to share their ratings with more evidence-based conversations.

- With a common observation rubric, participants can come together in their shared professional vision.

An Example

Step 1. The purpose for the video analysis is set. The facilitator tells participants that the focus of the VAT activity is to work on inter-rater agreement for a particular item, within a particular domain on an observation rubric—for instance, Domain 1: Planning and Preparation, Item 1b, Demonstrating Knowledge of Students, from the 2013 *Danielson Framework for Teaching* (https://www.nctq.org/dmsView/2016-2017_TEG_TEXT).

RUBRIC ANALYSIS

DOMAIN 1: PLANNING AND PREPARATION

1b Demonstrating Knowledge of Students

HIGHLY EFFECTIVE	EFFECTIVE
The teacher understands the active nature of student learning and acquires information about levels of development for individual students. The teacher also systematically acquires knowledge from several sources about individual student's varied approaches to learning, knowledge and skills, special needs and interests, and cultural heritages.	Teacher understands the active nature of student learning, and attains information about levels of development for groups of students. The teacher also purposefully acquires knowledge from several sources about groups of students' varied approaches to learning, knowledge and skills, special needs, and interests and cultural heritage.
CRITICAL ATTRIBUTES	**CRITICAL ATTRIBUTES**
In addition to the characteristics of "effective," • *The teacher uses ongoing methods to assess students' skill levels and designs instruction accordingly.* • *The teacher seeks out information about their cultural heritage from all students.* • *The teacher maintains a system of updated student records and incorporates medical and/or learning needs into lesson plans.*	• *The teacher knows, for groups of students, their levels of cognitive development.* • *The teacher is aware of the different cultural groups in the class.* • *The teacher has a good idea of the range of interests of students in the class.* • *The teacher has identified "high," "medium," and "low" groups of students within the class.* • *The teacher is well informed about students' cultural heritage and incorporates this knowledge in lesson planning.* • *The teacher is aware of the special needs represented by students in the class.*

(Continued)

(Continued)

POSSIBLE EXAMPLES	POSSIBLE EXAMPLES
• *The teacher plans his lesson with three different follow-up activities, designed to meet the varied ability levels of his students.* • *The teacher plans to provide multiple project options; students will self-select the project that best meets their individual approach to learning.* • *The teacher encourages students to be aware of their individual reading levels and make independent reading choices that will be challenging, but not too difficult.* • *The teacher attends the local Mexican heritage day, meeting several of his students' extended family members.* • *The teacher regularly creates adapted assessment materials for several students with learning disabilities.*	• *The teacher creates an assessment of students' levels of cognitive development.* • *The teacher examines previous year's cumulative folders to ascertain the proficiency levels of groups of students in the class.* • *The teacher administers a student interest survey at the beginning of the school year.* • *The teacher plans activities using his knowledge of students' interests.* • *The teacher knows that five of her students are in the Garden Club; she plans to have them discuss horticulture as part of the next biology lesson.* • *The teacher realizes that not all of his students are Christian, so he plans to read a Hanukah story in December.* • *The teacher plans to ask her Spanish-speaking students to discuss their ancestry as part of their Social Studies unit studying South America.*

DOMAIN 1: PLANNING AND PREPARATION

1b Demonstrating Knowledge of Students

DEVELOPING	INEFFECTIVE
Teacher indicates the importance of understanding how students learn and the students' backgrounds, cultures, skills, language proficiency, interests, and special needs, and attains this knowledge for the class as a whole.	Teacher demonstrates little or no understanding of how students learn, and little knowledge of students' backgrounds, cultures, skills, language proficiency, interests, and special needs, and does not seek such understanding.
CRITICAL ATTRIBUTES	CRITICAL ATTRIBUTES
• *Teacher cites developmental theory, but does not seek to integrate it into lesson planning.* • *Teacher is aware of the different ability levels in the class, but tends to teach to the "whole group."*	• *Teacher does not understand child development characteristics and has unrealistic expectations for students.* • *Teacher does not try to ascertain varied ability levels among students in the class.*

CRITICAL ATTRIBUTES	CRITICAL ATTRIBUTES
• The teacher recognizes that children have different interests and cultural backgrounds, but rarely draws on their contributions or differentiates materials to accommodate those differences. • The teacher is aware of medical issues and learning disabilities with some students, but does not seek to understand the implications of that knowledge.	• Teacher is not aware of student interests or cultural heritages. • Teacher takes no responsibility to learn about students' medical or learning disabilities.

POSSIBLE EXAMPLES	POSSIBLE EXAMPLES
• The teacher's lesson plan has the same assignment for the entire class, in spite of the fact that one activity is beyond the reach of some students. • In the unit on Mexico, the teacher has not incorporated perspectives from the three Mexican-American children in the class. • Lesson plans make only peripheral reference to students' interests. • The teacher knows that some of her students have IEPs but they're so long, she hasn't read them yet.	• The lesson plan includes a teacher presentation for an entire 30-minute period to a group of 7-year-olds. • The teacher plans to give her ELL students the same writing assignment she gives the rest of the class. • The teacher plans to teach his class Christmas carols, despite the fact that he has four religions represented amongst his students.

Step 2. Participants are asked to individually read the criteria for each level of the ratings, the critical attributes, and the possible examples for both effective and ineffective levels.

Step 3. Each participant would then do a six-step thinking protocol in writing about their concerns/thoughts about observing for this item.

1. What might you discuss in a PRE-observation conference to support the teacher's success in this area?

2. What might you observe for WHILE watching the lesson to find evidence for this area?

3. What might be a question asked in POST-observation conference that would bring out the teacher's thinking in this area?

4. What evidence could be collected other than observation data for this area?

5. What are concerns you have about being able to observe for this area? What would you need to know in advance about the learners before being able to assess this?

6. Do you believe this is a critical aspect of teacher effectiveness? Do you believe that if you do NOT find evidence of this practice in the teacher's observed lesson that the lesson should be rated lower because of its absence?

Step 4. The participants then form pairs and discuss their answers to these six items. They may strongly converge on questions 1 through 5, but item 6 is likely to lead to more of a values-based discussion. This type of "opinion about the rubric item" is usually avoided for that reason, yet our underlying beliefs form the lenses through which we see practice. It is important for observers to

(Continued)

(Continued)

become aware of their biases in order to observe more objectively and to collect more data than they might without this awareness. Many times observers avoid items or treat them superficially, because they do not believe in their worth; by hearing the opinions of valued colleagues in their field as well as those from other discipline areas, they may begin to see the importance of the particular observation focus.

Step 5. The facilitator engages the whole group in discussion of items 6, then 2, in that order. Item 2 is elaborated with "look-fors" from the group in the form of a shared list.

Step 6. Participants are asked to watch a 15-minute video from a local classroom, in which there IS evidence to be found of this practice. (As with all of these activities, the facilitator should try the complete activity first on their own with the video clip they plan to use to ensure it will be workable for the task.) Viewers are asked to watch the video with ONLY this particular item in mind. They are only seeking evidence for "demonstrating knowledge of students." As they watch, they are asked to jot down this evidence as descriptive notes on a provided form. This VAT task can be practiced using a video selected from this online resource: http://www.doe.mass.edu/edeval/resources/calibration/videos.html. When using videos retrieved from online sources, make sure to begin the video analysis task after any introductory text or commentary so as not to bias the viewers. Allowing participants to watch "raw" video is essential to all of these tasks. Downloading them from their source enables facilitators to edit them or trim away text and commentary and allows viewing without the labels or comments that might be found next to the video on the host site.

Step 7. After collecting their notes, participants are asked to pair up again and compare their notes.

Step 8. Each participant individually determines a rating for the observed teaching on the 1 to 4 scale (ineffective, developing, effective, highly effective).

Step 9. Participants share their ratings in pairs, groups, or with the whole group, as the facilitator clarifies their evidence and promotes interaction and discussion. The facilitator is prepared with the "accurate" rating based on prior work with principals and teachers so that participants do hear what rating would be given by their administrators.

Step 10. Participants are given a chance to return to reflect on the entire VAT activity with calibration as a focus, considering how their rating aligned with the "accurate" one. Usually both the facilitator and participants are simply amazed at how complex coming to calibration on just one item on a rubric can be. This ideally leads to more respect for the need for training and integrity in the process.

Optional Variations and Extensions

a. The process could be repeated with a new video sample and the same observation focus, until inter-rater agreement is reached. Inter-rater agreement should be reached after two to three rounds.

b. The process could be repeated with the same video sample but a new observation focus, again until inter-rater agreement is reached.

c. A full-length lesson video can be watched at home, and evaluators can score the whole lesson using the evaluation tool. They can submit their scores and receive feedback from evaluators who have already set the scores with commentary. Evaluators can compare their scores to the ones provided.

d. A full-length lesson video could be scored by evaluators from different disciplinary backgrounds—for instance, a math educator and a special educator. Their scores could be compared for insights into the data they capture for the various indicators on the evaluation tool.

Template to Guide VAT Activity

Calibration of Observers: Focus on Demonstrating Knowledge of Students

Examine the provided rubric document: Domain 1: Planning and Preparation, Item 1b, Demonstrating Knowledge of Students, from the 2013 *Danielson Framework for Teaching* (https://www.nctq.org/dmsView/2016-2017_TEG_TEXT). Individually, read through the criteria for each level of the ratings, the critical attributes, and the possible examples for both effective and ineffective levels.

Write about your concerns/thoughts about observing for this item.

Six-Step Thinking Protocol for Evaluation Criteria

- What might you discuss in a PRE-observation conference to support the teacher's success in this area?

- What might you observe for WHILE watching the lesson to find evidence for this area?

- What might be a question asked in POST-observation conference that would bring out the teacher's thinking in this area?

- What evidence could be collected other than observation data for this area?

- What are concerns you have about being able to observe for this area? What would you need to know in advance about the learners before being able to assess this?

- Do you believe this is a critical aspect of teacher effectiveness? Do you believe that if you do NOT find evidence of this practice in the teacher's observed lesson that the lesson should be rated lower because of its absence?

(Continued)

(Continued)

1. Form pairs and discuss your answers to these six items. Share with the whole group and specify your "look-fors" for question 2 of the six-step protocol.

2. Watch the video, and individually jot down any descriptive evidence of student or teacher behavior, actions, or language that could relate to the area of "demonstrating knowledge of students" as well as moments where you could imagine it being included but it did not occur.

3. Pair up and compare your notes with your partner's.

4. Individually provide a rating for the teaching you watched on the video from 1 through 4.

5. Share your rating with the group, and after discussion, see how the sample was rated by your administration.

6. Reflect on this video analysis task. What do you think you learned or reinforced about evaluation and calibration from participating in it?

VAT Activity 2. Self-Assessment via Video

Level of Activity

Advanced, suitable for experienced observers

Overview

When teachers only encounter external evaluation of their performance, they can unfortunately begin to perceive it as political enactment of control, conformity, or micromanagement rather than as a vehicle for professional development. Instead, inviting teachers to be evaluators of their own performance encourages them to be active agents in the process. Self-assessment has been found useful in guiding teachers to think about their own standards for quality teaching, helping them set goals for development, and improving their ability to communicate with peers in the profession (Ross & Bruce, 2007). When teachers heighten their awareness as to what takes place in the class-room and why it is taking place, they are in a better position to articulate their needs and determine the actions that are most likely to lead to improvement in their instructional practice. Video is the only tool through which teacher self-observation can occur, and it has shown positive results in pre-service teacher education as well as in the ongoing learning of experienced teachers (Sherin & van Es, 2005). When self-observation through video is done systematically among an entire faculty, with the support of administrators and other key stakeholders, it has the potential to bring about positive transformational change at the institutional level.

Support for self-evaluation in learning is based on theories of self-regulation as well as metacognition. Engaging teachers in the metacognitive task of stepping back to appraise their own performance stimulates self-monitoring. This encourages a more active and self-reliant role in one's own learning. Heightened self-awareness, leading to ever greater self-regulation, has been shown to yield benefits including a greater awareness of the evaluation process and scoring criteria, an increased understanding of the instructional content, and improved performance (Fallows & Chandramohan, 2001). Teachers who engage in self-evaluation within a collaborative culture that fosters trust, openness, and support will more likely find the motivation to develop professionally and may be more amenable to the idea of working to improve their practice than under more traditional approaches to teacher evaluation. Furthermore, when professional development initiatives are closely tied to clearly articulated processes for self-evaluation, it can foster self-reliance for ongoing learning.

Underlying Design Components

- Trying out a sample lesson with the observation criteria helps the teacher and supervisor jointly orient to the performance expectations.

- Using one component of an observation rubric rather than an entire one helps with the ability to focus more deeply on a target growth area.

- Knowing the observation criteria in advance and allowing the teacher to select a segment for use in self-assessment empowers the teacher in the process.

- Choosing to start with observation protocols that are not numeric scales but require tallying and coding keep the teacher focused on data collection rather than judgment.

- Supporting the use of description before evaluation (D comes before E) enables observers to share their ratings with more evidence-based conversations.

- With a common observation rubric, the supervisor and teacher can have a grounded conversation about the teacher's performance that is based on the teacher's rather than the supervisor's evaluation.

An Example

Step 1. The purpose for the video analysis is set. The teacher and supervisor are exploring self-assessment as a component of teacher performance evaluation as well as ongoing professional

(Continued)

(Continued)

development. They decide to build off their science department's observation protocol, focusing just on classroom discussion, the area that both the teacher and supervisor have agreed will be the teacher's growth area for the school year. They utilize a data collection protocol rather than a rating scale.

Target Area: Promoting Student Discussion in the Inquiry-Based Classroom	
Amount of time Observed:	
Percentage of students contributing to the discussion:	
Tally/Count/Code:	
Closed questions:	Open-ended questions:
Teacher questions:	Student questions:
Lower-order questions:	Higher-order questions:
Student speaks to teacher:	Student speaks to other student(s):
Teacher provides reasoning:	Teacher supports student reasoning:
Students do not use evidence for claims:	Students use evidence to support claims:

Step 2. After the supervisor and the teacher have discussed these criteria, ideally looking at some footage of another teacher to look for evidence as a practice observation, the teacher plans, teaches, and video captures a lesson with the intention of "putting their best foot forward." Knowing the observation criteria in advance in this way makes the observation process proactive rather than reactive. This gives the teacher the opportunity to strive toward a clear goal and be prepared for their self-assessment. Once the video is selected by the teacher, it is uploaded to a designated secure platform.

Step 3. After the video has been uploaded to a secure platform, the teacher watches the full-length lesson and takes notes with timestamps of any episodes in which they saw evidence of student discussion. After collecting this evidence, the teacher then marks each band of the criteria with tallies or evidence.

Step 4. The teacher completes the self-assessment by writing some reflections about the lesson video and their findings and sets further growth goals.

Step 5. The teacher and supervisor set a time to meet and for the teacher to share their self-assessment. They can watch portions of the video together, starting with segments (three to six minutes in length) that the teacher selects, or the supervisor can just listen and decide whether the video footage needs to be checked then or at another time. The supervisor's role is to try to better understand the teacher's thinking through the observations and reflections they share and to assess whether the evaluation appears to be accurate and the growth goals appropriate.

Step 6. Teachers are given a chance to return to reflect on the entire VAT activity.

Optional Variations and Extensions

a. Teachers can repeat the process consistently over a period of four to six weeks until they see the change in their performance.

b. Teachers can share self-assessments, using the same criteria, with colleagues for peer feedback as well as then sharing with a supervisor.

c. Additional categories from the observation protocol can then be examined in the same way until the entire instrument can be utilized over a series of lessons.

d. More expansive criteria for higher-order discussions can be examined, which can be more open-ended once teachers are experienced with low-inference note-taking, such as https://library.teachingworks.org/wp-content/uploads/Discussion_Decomposition.pdf.

Template to Guide VAT Activity

Self-Assessment via Video: Focus on Student Higher-Order Discussion

1. Examine the provided observation protocol, adapted from Discussion, from the *Fermilab Science Education Classroom Observation Protocol* (https://ed.fnal.gov/trc_new/program_docs/instru/classroom_obs.pdf). Teacher and supervisor read through the criteria for each level of the ratings and watch a sample video of another teacher to try looking for evidence of this practice.

2. After the supervisor and the teacher have discussed these criteria, ideally looking at footage of another teacher to look for evidence as a practice observation, the teacher plans, teaches, and video captures a lesson with the intention of showing student discussion as described in the observation protocol.

3. Once the video has been uploaded to a secure platform, the teacher watches the full-length lesson and takes notes with timestamps of any episodes in which they saw evidence of student discussion. After collecting this evidence, the teacher then marks each band of the criteria with tallies or evidence.

4. The teacher completes the self-assessment by writing some reflections about the lesson video and their findings and sets further growth goals, such as the following:

   - What surprised you? What did you learn?

   - What do you think about what your students are doing here?

   - What will you do differently next time? (Knight, 2014, p. 136)

5. The teacher and supervisor set up a time to video conference and share their evidence. The teacher goes first, and the supervisor adds in and helps ask clarifying questions. They do not share their ratings until after they have discussed the evidence. They then share their ratings and discuss whether either would change the rating based on their conversation and each other's evidence.

6. Reflect on this video analysis task. What do you think you learned or reinforced from participating in it?

VAT Activity 3. Distance Supervision

Level of Activity

Advanced, suitable for experienced observers

Overview

Within teacher education, the use of video to supervise teacher candidates long distance has been widely used and researched. This use arose to meet the needs of teachers enrolled in programs that are geographically remote because of a rural location of the participant teacher (Gruenhagen, Mccracken, & True, 1999), to offer supervision to teacher candidates participating in online programs, and to provide participation access to low-incidence programs, such as ones for teaching children with autism, which may be located in an area distant from the teacher candidate's home (Machalicek et al., 2010).

The use of video for distance supervision has moved into K–12 school districts that may not have supervisors with the expertise of the observed teacher. For instance, an article in the District Administration (https://districtadministration.com/a-clearer-view-of-the-classroom/) reports that video "allowed Newton County administrators to work with out-of-state consultants at Insight Education Group, who gave teachers long-distance math coaching that the district—which lacks a math coordinator—could not supply. The video-enabled coaching helped raise student scores on a statewide algebra exam." This example from a coaching perspective could also be applied to a viewer who assesses performance and offers suggestions for improvement, whether from a purely evaluative stance or one that is more developmental in nature. In both contexts—teacher education and K–12 school districts—these teachers' performance could only be evaluated from a distance through the medium of video.

Underlying Design Components

- Beginning with one aspect of the supervisory evaluation tool helps create a shared professional vision and calibrate the teacher and the supervisor. Because the supervisor is at a distance, they will not have any opportunity for informal visits or unplanned conversations to reach a shared understanding.

- Using observation protocols that have been researched, show evidence of validity and reliability is essential to ensuring that the distance supervision will be high quality and not bring in idiosyncratic or specious observation feedback.

- With a specific aspect of teaching to investigate, the conversation between the supervisor and the teacher stays more focused rather than moving to more sweeping evaluations.

- By focusing on the learners rather than the teacher in their first observation interactions, teachers may feel less defensive and more open to looking at their own practice as their conversations continue.

An Example

Step 1. The purpose for the video analysis is set. The teacher and mathematics supervisor, who is geographically removed from the school site, begin distance supervision by exploring the tool they will work with over the course of several months, the *Mathematics Classroom Observation Protocol for Practices* (MCOP2, Gleason, Livers, & Zelkowski, 2015). The tool is not designed to be used in its entirety in one lesson, and multiple lesson observations are needed. The teacher and supervisor review one area on the protocol that measures the degree of student engagement in exploration, investigation, or problem-solving, as opposed to following procedures. A description of this feature is discussed, preferably with an example and a non-example from the rubric designer:

Example: "In order for students to develop a flexible use of mathematics, they must be allowed to engage in exploration, investigation, and/or problem solving activities which go beyond following procedures presented by the teacher" (Gleason, Livers, & Zelkowski, 2015, p. 4).

Non-Example: "If students are following a procedure established by the teacher, then it does not count as exploration/investigation/problem solving. Instead, students should be determining their own solution pathway without necessarily knowing that the path will lead to the desired result" (Gleason, Livers, & Zelkowski, 2015, p. 4).

Score	Description
3	Students regularly engaged in exploration, investigation, or problem-solving. Over the course of the lesson, the majority of the students engaged in exploration/investigation/problem-solving.
2	Students sometimes engaged in exploration, investigation, or problem-solving. Several students engaged in problem-solving, but not the majority of the class.
1	Students seldom engaged in exploration, investigation, or problem-solving. This tended to be limited to one or a few students engaged in problem-solving while other students watched but did not actively participate.
0	Students did not engage in exploration, investigation, or problem-solving. There were either no instances of investigation or problem-solving, or the instances were carried out by the teacher without active participation by any students.

Step 2. After the supervisor and the teacher have discussed these criteria, ideally looking at some footage of another teacher to look for evidence as a practice observation, the teacher plans, teaches, and video captures a lesson with the intention of "putting their best foot forward." Knowing the observation criteria in advance in this way makes the observation process proactive rather than reactive. This gives the teacher the opportunity to strive toward a clear goal and for the supervisor to assess the teacher's areas of strengths and areas for growth. Once the video is selected by the teacher, it is uploaded to the designated shared platform.

Step 3. After the video has been uploaded to a secure platform, both the teacher and the supervisor watch the full-length lesson and take notes with timestamps of any episodes in which they saw evidence of student engagement in exploration, investigation, or problem-solving. After collecting this evidence, they each decide on a score (0–3) from the MCOP2.

Step 4. The teacher and supervisor set a time to meet via video conference to discuss the lesson, where they can also watch portions of the video. They can watch portions of the video together, starting with segments (three to six minutes in length) that the teacher selects and then segments that the supervisor suggests watching. The supervisor's role is to try to better understand the teacher's thinking through the observations and reflections they share and to not jump in too soon with their own evidence or rating. They then share their ratings and discuss whether either would change it based on their conversation and each other's evidence.

Step 5. Teachers are given a chance to return to reflect on the entire VAT activity with student engagement in mathematical investigation, exploration, and problem-solving as a focus.

Optional Variations and Extensions

a. Teachers and supervisors could watch the video for the first time together, if there isn't time for them to preview it separately beforehand, and stop to discuss evidence as they see it emerging. They can jointly score the video using the protocol.

b. Instead of a whole lesson video with one criteria, a shorter clip could be used to first establish the process of finding descriptive evidence.

c. Teacher and supervisor first do this task on another teacher's video, not the teacher's own, to establish the process.

d. Additional categories from the observation protocol can then be examined in the same way until the entire instrument can be utilized over a series of lessons.

Template to Guide VAT Activity

Distance Supervision: Focus on Student Engagement in Mathematics

1. Examine the provided observation protocol: Student Engagement, from the *Mathematics Classroom Observation Protocol for Practices* (http://jgleason.people.ua.edu/mcop2.html). Teacher and supervisor read through the criteria for each level of the ratings and watch a sample video of another teacher to try looking for evidence of this practice.

2. After the supervisor and the teacher have discussed these criteria, ideally looking at some footage of another teacher to look for evidence as a practice observation, the teacher plans, teaches, and video captures a lesson with the intention of showing student engagement as described in the observation protocol.

3. The teacher and the supervisor watch the full-length lesson and take notes with timestamps of any episodes in which they saw evidence of student engagement in exploration, investigation, or problem-solving. After collecting this evidence, they each decide on a score (0–3) from the MCOP2.

4. The teacher and supervisor set up a time to video conference and share their evidence. The teacher goes first, and the supervisor adds in and helps ask clarifying questions. They do not share their ratings until after they have discussed the evidence. They then share their ratings and discuss whether either would change it based on their conversation and each other's evidence.

5. Reflect on this video analysis task. What do you think you learned or reinforced about evaluation and calibration from participating in it?

VAT Activity 4. Video in Teacher Portfolios

Level of Activity

Advanced, suitable for experienced observers

Overview

One of the ways video can be used as a component of teacher evaluation is as an artifact within a portfolio that is used to support teacher reflection on their own and their students' learning. An electronic portfolio is a digitized collection of evidence of teacher practice and can incorporate documents like lesson plans, student work samples, self- and supervisor-evaluations, reflective writing, as well as media such as video, photos, or audio. Meaningful portfolio development is based on the teacher's analysis on the evidence and authenticity in demonstrating what has been achieved as well as growth goals. The process of creating it—rather than the portfolio itself—is the professional learning (Tarrant, 2013).

This process of developing their portfolios has demonstrated positive effects on teacher identity, knowledge, skills, reflection and technology as well as on self-regulation, self-efficacy, and self-evaluation (Kilbane & Milman, 2017). Among the artifacts usually collected for ePortfolios, videos in particular have the potential to be powerful mediating objects, by grounding teacher's reflection and offering them the chance to document their progress by looking at baseline and subsequent performance evidence. In their study of video artifacts in teacher's ePortfolios, Shepherd and Hannafin (2008) found that the inclusion of video facilitated reflection-supported inquiry into classroom practice and influenced self-improvement plans.

Underlying Design Components

- Providing a sample from another teacher helps set clear expectations for the reflective writing expected.

- Using structured prompts aligned to a domain on a local teacher evaluation protocol ensures that the contents of the video analysis and all the reflective documents in the portfolio stay connected to standards.

- Enabling teachers to submit video clips rather than full-length lessons allows them to zoom in on particular moments of instruction they wish to explore or to showcase.

An Example

Step 1. The purpose for the video analysis is set. The teacher is provided with the structured prompts for completing their reflection on a video artifact, such as the one below developed to corresponding to Component 4A, reflecting on teaching, from the 2013 *Danielson Framework for Teaching* (https://www.nctq.org/dmsView/2016-2017_TEG_TEXT).

Template for Commentary on Video Artifact

Danielson Framework Component 4a—Reflecting on Teaching

Background to this reflection	What is the context for this reflection on your practice?
Planning or instructional practice focus of this reflection	What in particular is your focus, in terms of planning and instruction?

(Continued)

(Continued)

Observing the instruction	What can be seen going on in this video clip?
Promoting a positive learning environment	How does the clip show your interaction with students in terms of respect, responsiveness, and challenge?
Developing the content-area skill	How does this clip show students deepening their understanding of the content?
Engaging students in communication	How does this clip show students interacting in discussion about the learning point?
Wonderings	What did you notice that makes you want to make changes to your practice?
Possible next steps in my practice	What changes would you make to your instruction—for the whole class and/or for students who need greater support or challenge?

Step 2. The teacher is provided a sample completed commentary with the video artifact, which is a clip about four to five minutes in length. This VAT can be practiced using this video, at http://vimeo.com/84320494 (Password: Video Analysis). The sample completed template below is based on that video.

Sample Completed Template for Commentary on Video Artifact

Danielson Framework Component 4a—Reflecting on Teaching

Background and goal of this reflection	**What is the context for this reflection on your practice?** For example *As a participant in a Video Learning Community at my school, I chose to examine my questioning techniques in terms of how they could better draw out student responses. My learners are beginning-level English as a Second language students and, while I am working to provide access to the content curriculum, I am also trying to expand their language skills.*
Planning or instructional practice focus	**What in particular is your focus, in terms of planning and instruction?** For example *In this lesson I was reviewing their comprehension of the first part of a short story by Jack London, "The Story of Keesh," that I had adapted to their language level, as well as asking them to apply a common core skill, that of choosing good evidence to support a claim. I wanted to refine their use of the vocabulary items "to be determined" and "to be clever" in order to help them use them more appropriately, since both terms were ones I would be using a lot in describing this character in this unit.*
Observing the instruction	**What can be seen going on in this video clip?** For example *In this clip, I am asking students to look at the smartboard where I had projected a number of statements that were all true from the story. Some of the statements*

could be used as evidence that the main character, Keesh, was determined, while others were better as evidence that Keesh was clever. Students raised their hands to respond and were then asked to explain their reasoning. In this video clip, three students can be heard responding.

Promoting a positive learning environment	**How does the clip show your interaction with students in terms of respect, responsiveness, and challenge?**

For example

I noticed that I was modifying my speech in terms of speed, word choice, and enunciation, which was intentional given that the learners are at beginning to low-intermediate levels of English proficiency and most have been in the country less than two years. I also saw that when the first student attempted to answer but read the letter of the response rather than reading out the full sentence, I asked her to go back in a way that showed patience. In terms of challenge, I saw that the activity was one that caused them to apply their knowledge of the story's main character through the lens of determination and cleverness, which are closely related concepts and therefore posed some difficulty in teasing apart.

Developing the content-area skill	**How does this clip show students deepening their understanding of the content?**

For example

Prior to this lesson, students had participated in a Readers' Theater version of "The Story of Keesh" in order to make it more comprehensible. This appeared to have brought clarity to them in terms of the plot and the characters. However, to deepen their critical thinking about which aspects of the story were designed by the author to suggest that Keesh survived, not only because he was determined but also because he was clever, I provided a series of claims that were all true from the story. I gave them claims such as "Keesh's father was a great hunter" and "Keesh put a small bone inside the meat." Students' choice of responses was limited to "that is evidence he is clever, or that is evidence that he is determined." This caused them to go beyond the plotting and characters to discern best evidence, which is a nuanced skill. All of the students needed to complete this activity on their own papers working independently as I circulated. Twenty-five out of 32 students had written down answers at the point this clip begins, with an average accuracy of about 80% prior to reviewing the responses as a whole class.

Engaging students in communication	**How does this clip show students interacting in discussion about the learning point?**

For example

In this clip, there are several practices I noticed that appeared to engage students in more extended responses. Students were given time, prior to the video clip, to review the statements on the smartboard and decide if they were good evidence of him being determined or being clever. Students sat in small groups and were able to talk with peers at their table using their native language or English to talk over their ideas while I circulated. When the clip starts, you see me beginning to ask for answers. Several hands were raised for each of the statements. I believe because I asked "Why?" students then needed to construct longer replies. I also resisted giving my "correct" answer too soon to encourage more talk about each item. For example, when the boy in the front was asked to explain why he thought the

(Continued)

(Continued)

	statement was evidence for Keesh being determined, he replied, "Keesh is determined because he stands up to the gray-beards in the council even though he is a young boy." This student used the language from the story, "gray-beards" to describe when Keesh defies the council elders.
Wonderings	**What did you notice that makes you want to make changes to your practice?** For example *Although I attempted with the processing time, group format, and "Why" questioning to engage students in more talk, I wonder if it could have been richer and more inclusive of more student participants. While I know these are beginner/ low-intermediate ESL students and much of the talk is teacher-student, I wonder how I could have structured the activity to promote more talk from more learners. I also wonder if they were truly needing to use the target forms "to be determined" and "to be clever" in their responses. I wonder how many students who hadn't responded really understood why those statements were evidence for " clever" or "determined."*
Possible next steps in my practice	**What changes would you make to your instruction—for the whole class and/or for students who need greater support or challenge?** For example *I believe that in order for students to participate more fully, I needed to have asked students to, not only identify their ideas in advance of reviewing them as a whole class, but to have gone back after the share out and asked students to pick 1 statement and explain why it was or was not good evidence. Advanced students could have explained two or three of the claims. I will ask students to "post" write after my next whole-class share out to have better evidence of what individual students understood. Another idea I plan to try is to have students practice reviewing the answers in their group, perhaps in a clockwise rotation so everyone speaks. Each student could say what they thought the answer was, with the student to the left asking "Why is that good evidence?" and the first student would have a chance to try and explain. This would give these ELLs a lot more practice with providing a more extended response prior to my calling for a share out in front of the whole class and being asked for an extended response cold. Each of these possible steps could enhance students' comprehension of the content and extend their language skills.*

Step 3. Follow-up steps could include connecting this video artifact to others in the portfolio, sharing it with a supervisor or with colleagues, and revisiting it with a follow-up video analysis on the same topic to look for improvement.

Optional Variations and Extensions

a. Teachers can repeatedly examine a core practice, like questioning and discussion techniques, over the course of a school year and use video to support this thread of investigation.

b. Instead of a short clip, a whole lesson could be included with a self-evaluation rubric as well as responses to open-ended prompts.

c. Teachers could meet in professional-learning communities to share their goals, discoveries, and complexities of teaching they are discovering as they build their portfolio.

PUTTING IDEAS INTO ACTION

Looking across the ideas and activities presented in this chapter, consider the following questions:

1. What do you see as common features across all four video analysis activities in this chapter?

2. What skills for video viewing might teachers/coaches/supervisors develop if they completed these activities?

3. What do you anticipate as problematic, new, or uncomfortable if you were trying these activities out with participants?

4. In what ways could these activities be set up in an online, self-paced format?

5. Which parts of this chapter resonate for you in terms of facilitating other educators' conversations or for your own use of video analysis?

Chapter References

Colorado Department of Education. (n.d.). *A guide to developing evaluation practices.* Retrieved from https://www.cde.state.co.us/educatoreffectiveness/iraguide

Fallows, S., & Chandramohan, B. (2001). Multiple approaches to assessment: Reflections on use of tutor, peer and self-assessment. *Teaching in Higher Education, 6*(2), 229–245.

Gleason, J., Livers, S. D., & Zelkowski, J. (2015). *Mathematics classroom observation protocol for practices: Descriptors manual.* Retrieved from http://jgleason.people.ua.edu/mcop2.html

Graham, M., Milanowski, A., & Miller, J. (2012). *Measuring and promoting inter-rater agreement of teacher and principal performance ratings.* Center for Educator Compensation and Reform. Retrieved from https://files.eric.ed.gov/fulltext/ED532068.pdf

Gruenhagen, K., Mccracken, T., & True, J. (1999). Using distance education technologies for the supervision of student teachers in remote rural schools. *Rural Special Education Quarterly, 18*(3–4), 58–65.

Kane, T., Gehlbach, H., Greenburg, M., Quinn, D., & Thal, D. (2015). *The best foot forward project: Substituting teacher-collected video for in-person classroom observations first year implementation report.* Center for Education Policy Research, Harvard University. Retrieved from http://cepr.harvard.edu/files/cepr/files/l4a_best_foot_forward_research_brief1.pdf

Kilbane, C. R., & Milman, N. B. (2017). Examining the impact of the creation of digital portfolios by high school teachers and their students on teaching and learning. *International Journal of ePortfolio, 7*(1), 101–109.

Knight, J. (2014). *Focus on teaching.* Corwin Press.

Machalicek, W., O'Reilly, M. F., Rispoli, M., Davis, T., Lang, R., Franco, J. H., & Chan, J. M. (2010). Training teachers to assess the challenging behaviors of students with autism using video tele-conferencing. *Education and Training in Autism and Developmental Disabilities,* 203–215.

Ross, J. A., & Bruce, C. D. (2007). Teacher self-assessment: A mechanism for facilitating professional growth. *Teaching and Teacher Education, 23*(2), 146–159.

Shepherd, C. E., & Hannafin, M. J. (2008). Examining preservice teacher inquiry through video-based, formative assessment e-portfolios. *Journal of Computing in Teacher Education, 25*(1), 31–37.

Sherin, M., & van Es, E. (2005). Using video to support teachers' ability to notice classroom interactions. *Journal of Technology and Teacher Education, 13*(3), 475–491.

Southern Regional Education Board. (2015, February). *Toward trustworthy and transformative classroom observations* (SREB's educator effectiveness series). Retrieved from https://www.sreb.org/sites/main/files/file-attachments/sreb_coreportonline.pdf

Tarrant, P. (2013). *Reflective practice and professional development*. London, United Kingdom: Sage.

Whitehurst, J., Chingos, M. M., & Lindquist, K. M. (2014). *Evaluating teachers with classroom observations—Lessons learned in four districts*. Washington, DC: Brown Center on Education Policy at Brookings.

10

CREATING A VIDEO
LIBRARY OF TEACHING

What a school thinks about its library is a measure
of what it feels about education.

—Harold Howe (1967)

CHAPTER OBJECTIVES

- To emphasize the importance of developing a personal, professional video library of teaching and the selection of video materials

- To suggest three routes to creating a video library of teaching: creating, cultivating, and curating

- To provide approaches to housing and storing a video library for optimum usability

An infinite variety of learning activities, professional dialogues, and tasks can be designed using video records of teaching as a material. Finding just the right video, however, can be really challenging and time-consuming. In Chapter 4, some of the limitations of video resources that are freely available online were described, such as the fit of the video with the local teaching context, locating videos that have the content needed for the professional development topic, or just finding authentic, unedited clips of unstaged teaching. These limitations make creating one's own videos essential. Video that is created by teachers to use in coaching or supervisory contexts can become part of a collection that is later used for professional learning tasks.

In this chapter, two additional approaches are outlined for developing a useful set of video clips connected to the video analysis tasks described in Chapters 5 through 9: curating available video and cultivating one's own collection to develop a video library of teaching. In addition, suggestions about how these videos can best be archived and made accessible and retrievable will be provided.

DEVELOPING A VIDEO LIBRARY OF TEACHING

Effective professional development for teachers depends upon designing tasks that will truly engage their thinking and motivate them to examine their practice. Video materials greatly enhance these activities but can be more difficult to readily access than other artifacts, such as student work samples, curriculum materials, or lesson plans. For teacher leaders, coaches, and all those involved in teacher education, professional learning activities can often be inspired by a particular video material, and conversely, video selection can also be done based once the focus of an activity has been set. While users and uses will vary, a video library can become a highly useful resource in facilitating teacher learning. Several tips should be kept in mind when building a video library of teaching.

A VIDEO LIBRARY

- Is a digital collection of classroom videos intended for use in professional learning

- Can be housed on a variety of online platforms but must be password protected, able to store and stream large files, easy to manage, and it should not be intimidating for users

- Should be tagged with a consistent lexicon so that search and retrieval is easier

- May be designed so that text materials, such as downloadable lesson plans, discussion questions, and student work, can be archived along with the video

- Is best maintained by a single individual or group utilizing a set of criteria to vet the video for quality control and to tag/label the entries for consistency in searches

- Could consist of locally produced video as well as curated, open-access videos

- Can allow for viewers to post their responses, notes, or to complete associated rubrics

Five reasons why facilitators of teacher learning would want to develop their own video libraries include the following:

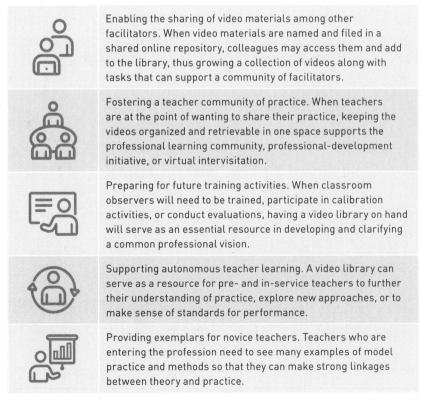

icons from https://iStock.com/Yuttapong

Enabling the sharing of video materials among other facilitators. When video materials are named and filed in a shared online repository, colleagues may access them and add to the library, thus growing a collection of videos along with tasks that can support a community of facilitators.

Fostering a teacher community of practice. When teachers are at the point of wanting to share their practice, keeping the videos organized and retrievable in one space supports the professional learning community, professional-development initiative, or virtual intervisitation.

Preparing for future training activities. When classroom observers will need to be trained, participate in calibration activities, or conduct evaluations, having a video library on hand will serve as an essential resource in developing and clarifying a common professional vision.

Supporting autonomous teacher learning. A video library can serve as a resource for pre- and in-service teachers to further their understanding of practice, explore new approaches, or to make sense of standards for performance.

Providing exemplars for novice teachers. Teachers who are entering the profession need to see many examples of model practice and methods so that they can make strong linkages between theory and practice.

SIX CONSIDERATIONS IN SELECTING VIDEO MATERIALS FOR USE IN TEACHER LEARNING

Keeping teacher learning goals in mind, a number of factors will influence the type of video material that might work best. Figure 1 below outlines some possible guidelines for the selection of video materials—which may seem readily apparent—that are important in optimizing teacher learning outcomes.

Content that aligns with the learning goals for a video analysis task can be difficult to come by through web searching. For instance, if a group of teachers wishes to explore approaches to use with students who are English language learners, there may be some video to be found online, but more likely finding the "right" video will require extensive searching and still not be exactly what fits the task. Producing video from local classrooms, with a local teacher who is skilled in teaching English learners, is often much more efficient. One way to carry this out is for a facilitator to work with the teacher and clearly specify a strategy they wish to view, and then the teacher incorporates that strategy into a routine lesson, capturing it on video. Another approach could be to provide a teacher with a list of strategies or work with them on a week's worth of lessons, building the strategies into the plans. Then, the lessons could be video recorded and reviewed by the facilitator, who would know where to look for those strategies and be able to edit out video clips that would work for their purposes.

FIGURE 10.1 ■ **Video selection criteria**

Content: Video of particular methods, teacher moves, or situations, in particular grade levels or content areas

Artifacts: Video is accompanied by lesson plans, student work samples, transcripts, or other supporting documents

Context: Video of young learners, adolescents, adults, and taken from urban, suburban, or rural schools

Audio: Video has very clear audio of student and teacher speech, or audio is not as important

Length: Video clips of three, five, eight minutes, full lessons of 20 through 35 minutes, or segments of video connected over the story arc of a lesson or unit

Angle: Video taken of whole class, small groups, or from student/teacher vantage point

Context has been shown to be an important variable in the authenticity of video analysis. Teachers are often more open to and willing to analyze and explore teaching in video from contexts that resemble their own. As mentioned with the challenge of finding the right content online, finding a context that looks like one's own schools is much more readily accomplished by filming in local schools. Teachers notice many aspects, such as room architecture, classroom furniture, the age, style of dress, ethnicity of pupils and teachers, regional accents, and other features that can either help them relate to the context or keep it at arm's length.

Length of video is another aspect to consider. In general, the match of the task to the length of viewing should take into account the intensity and frequency required. For instance, if participants are asked to tally teacher questions and there are many within a particular five-minute episode of teaching, reviewing this clip three times makes more sense than showing a 15-minute clip. The rewind/review possibilities of watching video clips works effectively when participants need to capture specific elements of classroom interaction. In contrast, viewers may need to see the whole lesson or longer segments to assess the lesson on a comprehensive rubric. To examine the implementation of a unit of study, multiple clips taken over a week's worth of lessons may make sense.

Angle of view can be relevant, depending on the viewing task that is being planned. For instance, if the viewing task involves participants looking at movement patterns of the teacher around the room, this circulation is best seen if the camera is set up on high and far enough back to capture the whole room. If watching the way in which a student works through a math task using manipulatives is important, then the video should be captured close up and over the student's shoulder to see their work at the table.

Audio quality is actually one of the aspects in analyzing video that becomes very important and yet is not always considered when first looking for video materials. For instance, when the video observation task requires viewers to capture and transcribe student talk and it is inaudible, the task becomes very frustrating. On the other hand, if the task requires a classroom mapping or marking of movement patterns, the audio quality will not be a relevant feature of the material. In fact, many observation tasks work well when the audio is turned off—for example, when viewers are asked to simply watch body language, transitions, or the teacher's board work. Others work well when the video is turned off but participants only hear the audio—for example, to record student-teacher talk. In that case, the audio quality should be very good, or audio records, instead of video, can be used.

Artifacts, such as lesson plans, student work samples, rubrics, or transcripts that accompany the video, make that material much more useful for professional development purposes. For example, given the choice between two clips—where one is accompanied by (1) information about the students, (2) a school context document, and (3) the teacher's lesson plan and another clip that has none of those artifacts—it makes sense to pick the former. Often viewers want to know more about the background of the teacher, school, learners, or curriculum, and having that information can offer a grounding to video analysis. When video is being captured in local contexts for future teacher-learning sessions, it is very practical and forward-thinking to simultaneously collect or create these artifacts.

CREATING, CULTIVATING, AND CURATING A COLLECTION OF VIDEO RECORDS OF TEACHING

There are three ways to build up a video library of teaching: creating, cultivating, and curating. Creation is maintaining a system to archive videos that teachers create as part of their participation in professional learning communities or through coaching/supervision. Cultivation refers to purposefully shooting and saving videos for future use from experienced and skilled local teachers, and curation involves locating already accessible videos that will be useful to the particular educator community.

→ Creating is a process of storing videos that had been locally made for various professional learning purposes with tagging that makes them easily retrievable.

→ Cultivating is a process of identifying the types of videos needed, purposefully finding local teachers willing to film for those practices, editing and selecting those that will be most useful, then storing them with tagging that makes them easily retrievable.

→ Curating is a process of identifying the types of videos sought after, searching for those videos online and within one's institution, and vetting them for quality, usability, and then storing them with tagging that makes them easily retrievable.

A video library can ideally consist of video records that have been locally produced as well as those that have been curated from preexisting collections.

Curating Videos From Web-Based Resources

Searching for videos with narrow search terms aids in the process but still requires time and patience. Many of the videos that are discoverable online are not very useful because of the nature of the content or the quality of the audio/video. There are more and more videos appearing, however, and the following criteria can help hone in on ones that will be most effective in teacher professional development.

Criteria for Selecting Videos Available Online	
Probably Eliminate	**Probably Keep**
• Audio very difficult to comprehend	• Comprehensible audio
• Video unclear/shaky	• Video clear and steady
• Video is mostly discussion about the lesson rather than seeing the lesson itself	• At least five minutes of raw, unedited classroom footage
• Video edited so that there is less than five minutes of uninterrupted footage of teaching	• Classroom practice fits the professional development focus
	• Classroom setting mirrors the local one

Criteria for Selecting Videos Available Online	
Probably Eliminate	**Probably Keep**
• Video is clearly staged or scripted and seems inauthentic • Hard to decide how it would be used for the professional development focus at hand • Classroom setting very different from local one	• Student-to-student talk can be heard • Is accompanied by context for learning information, such as grade level, program type, student profile • Is accompanied by other documents, like lesson plans, rubrics, coaches' reactions

Sites to Search for Videos of Teaching

One of the biggest challenges with finding really useful video footage of classrooms online is that most of the video is so heavily edited and interwoven with footage of the teacher talking about the teaching or overuse of titles floating on the picture that it is unusable for video analysis activities. These videos are really more designed as promotional or tutorial for particular approaches, such as the ones on Edutopia (https://www.edutopia.org/videos).

Other sites have a lot of potential to find unedited classroom footage, but there are still many in these collections that are teachers talking about teaching rather than the actual teaching, such as the Teaching Channel (https://www.teachingchannel.org/) and TeacherTube (https://www.teachertube.com/). These are worth looking through but with the caveat that most of the videos will not be uninterrupted footage and there may be advertisements.

The following sites are possible sources for curating videos of teaching that fit the selection criteria and might be a good place to start to look for videos. The ten sample sites included are only those that do not charge a fee, although some may require creating an account. This list is annotated with brief information about the kinds of clips that can be found, the age or content area, the developer of the video library, and any additional features that are notable about the collection. Within the collections, some are full-lesson length videos, but many are short clips, so length should be noted when choosing from these collections.

Selected List of Sites With Videos of Teaching

Site Address and Overview	Focus Area(s)	Grade Level	Special Features/ Materials	Creator/ Developer	Size of Collection
https:// highqualityearlylearning .org/ *"The High Quality Early Learning Project conducts* and communicates research about teaching that supports effective learning for young children and their families."	Early childhood education	PreK through 2	Discussion questions tied to each video are provided	City College of New York and the High Quality Early Learning Project	About 20 videos, some are teacher interviews

(Continued)

(Continued)

Site Address and Overview	Focus Area(s)	Grade Level	Special Features/ Materials	Creator/ Developer	Size of Collection
https://tle.soe.umich.edu/ "The Teaching & Learning Exploratory (TLE) based at the University of Michigan School of Education provides access to online resources that support the study of teaching and learning practices. The TLE disseminates these resources to the broad professional community of education professionals. The TLE contains videos of classroom lessons with data and teacher-provided classroom materials."	Math, literacy	1 through 9	Brief overview of lesson objectives	University of Michigan, School of Education	About 75 under free "Preview Videos" access area; More than 3,000 for paid subscription
http://www .insidemathematics.org/ classroom-videos "Learning from the practices of others is a powerful way to improve teaching. Here, you can explore real mathematics teaching and learning by exploring everyday classrooms where educators are working to refine their mathematics teaching practices."	Math	1 through 12	Lesson plans, materials, and student work samples are included as well as clips from cycles of teaching and re-teaching	University of Texas, Austin, and the Silicon Valley Mathematics Initiative	More than 35 videos
http://www.doe.mass .edu/edeval/resources/ calibration/videos.html "These videos depict a *range* of practice to support within-district calibration activities that promote a shared understanding of instructional quality. Select the video(s) that best meet your needs by grade, content area, or length."	ELA, math, science, social studies	1 through 12	Designed to support calibration activities among scorers of teacher performance rubrics	Massachusetts Department of Education	More than 40 videos

Site Address and Overview	Focus Area(s)	Grade Level	Special Features/ Materials	Creator/ Developer	Size of Collection
https://www.engageny .org/content/danielsons-framework-teaching-rubric-videos "The New York State Education Department provides videos of effective teacher practice aligned to Danielson's Framework for Teaching Rubric. Click on a Video Album link below to view examples of effective teacher practice."	All subjects possibly, but the videos are labeled by rubric criteria rather than subject or grade	K through 12	Designed to provide exemplar practices keyed to the Danielson Framework teacher performance rubric	New York State Department of Education	More than 60 videos
https://www .nextgenscience.org/ news/new-classroom-videos-demonstrating-transitions-ngss "The featured classroom examples illustrate how some educators are transitioning instruction to help students meet the goals of the NGSS. These videos are not intended to signal a one-size-fits-all approach to implementing the NGSS. Rather, the snapshots demonstrate how specific teachers are beginning to transition to the standards and offer guidance to educators currently considering how to best engage students in three-dimensional learning."	Science	2 through 5 and 9 through 12	Provides an introduction to how the new science standards look in action; transcripts are provided of the lessons, but there is a teacher interview injected which would need to be removed	Next Generation Science Standards/ videos hosted through the Teaching Channel	4 videos
https://www .montgomeryschoolsmd .org/departments/ development/resources/ video/ "Over the past few years, MCPS has developed staff development video resources to	All subjects, including Spanish, ESL, art	K through 12	A lesson overview is provided by the teacher on one video clip, and the lessons are broken up into labeled shorter clips	Montgomery County Public Schools, Maryland	More than 40 videos, many are complete lessons

(Continued)

(Continued)

Site Address and Overview	Focus Area(s)	Grade Level	Special Features/ Materials	Creator/ Developer	Size of Collection
illustrate best practices in effective teaching. The videos range from complete model lessons broken into segments with guiding questions, support material, and teacher reflections, to highlights of lessons that illustrate specific strategies and practices such as activators, summarizers, or equitable teaching strategies."					
https://achievethecore .org/teachingthecore "This collection of classroom videos and associated lesson materials was developed in 2013 to support K–12 educators implementing the Common Core State Standards. As all of the participants were at that time early in their own work with those standards, these videos were not intended to be exemplars. Rather, they showed real-life classrooms, with all the real-life challenges and successes found therein."	ELA, math, social studies	K through 12	Lesson plans, teacher interviews, student work, and guiding questions all connected to instructional practices for teaching the Common Core	Teaching the Core, funded by The Leona M. and Harry B. Helmsley Charitable Trust	More than 60 videos, and Supplemental videos area has additional 15 video cases
https://people.stanford .edu/claudeg/video/ classroom-videos "CQELL (Classroom Qualities for English Language Learners) is an observational instrument developed to conduct research with elementary-school English language learners (ELLs) during English language arts instruction."	ELA with English learners	K through 5	An observation protocol linked to moments in the video collection	Stanford Graduate School of Education	10 videos

Site Address and Overview	Focus Area(s)	Grade Level	Special Features/ Materials	Creator/ Developer	Size of Collection
https://rpm.fpg.unc.edu/resource-search?f%5B0%5D=field_resource_type%3A3 "Early Childhood Recommended Practice Modules (RPMs) are free modules developed for early care and education, early intervention, and early childhood special education faculty and professional development providers. The modules support the implementation of the Division for Early Childhood (DEC) Recommended Practices."	Early learning	Birth through age 5	Videos are embedded into learning modules about the DEC recommended practices	Early Childhood Recommended Practices (RPM) partners	About 50 videos, most of which are in home settings with caregivers but a number are with teachers
https://eleducation.org/resources/pd-packs/coaching-for-change "EL Education acknowledges the importance of conversations about teaching and learning as a critical component of the coaching cycle. We believe that the purpose for delivering feedback should always be to positively influence student learning."	Teacher coaching	Coaches	With instructive articles, discussion questions, and protocols, this part of the site offers videos of coaches giving feedback	Expeditionary Learning	Some coaching videos and some K through 12 teaching videos in this site

Cultivating Videos From Local, Experienced Teachers

Searching for preexisting videos can often surface a number of useful video records, but many times there just might not be that "right" video that would be ideal for a particular professional development activity. In those instances, it is far less time consuming and much more useful to proactively create a particular practice to be filmed. This can be carried out in several steps, outlined below.

Sample Scenario: Five Suggestions for Creating Customized Videos	
Steps	**Example**
Step 1: Identify the type of video that would work well for the professional development activity.	Ms. Rodriguez, a school-based facilitator, wishes to lead a session on strategies for teaching science content to English language learners with a group of teachers in a PLC.

(Continued)

(Continued)

Sample Scenario: Five Suggestions for Creating Customized Videos	
Steps	**Example**
Step 2: If nothing is readily available/appropriate via online resources, consider the options for filming a video clip to share in the activity.	Ms. Rodriguez has looked online but has not found the right type of video to use. She turns to several teachers she knows to ask if any of them would be willing to work with her on a lesson that she could video. At first none at her school site feel ready to do this, but she knows of a science teacher, Ms. Jones, from a nearby school in the same district she has worked with professionally who is happy to help.
Step 3: Once a teacher has volunteered to assist, seek out an honorarium if possible. Then, work with the teacher to tell them exactly which practices, situations, or scenes are desired in the video. Take time beforehand with the lesson plan to plan purposefully so such scenes can be captured.	Ms. Jones is interested in helping out, and Ms. Rodriguez is able to gain a $50 gift card to honor her time and support. They set up a time to speak, and during their conversation, Ms. Rodriguez explains that she is looking to capture a regular science lesson that Ms. Jones would normally be teaching that week, but she specifies that she is looking to capture the following two practices: (1) use of visuals to create access to the lesson content and (2) linguistic supports for students to speak to peers during a turn and talk. They discuss the lesson and how and when Ms. Jones imagines those practices would occur.
Step 4: Determine who, when, and how the video will be recorded. Ensure that the focus teacher has signed permission forms from all the pupils and has signed one as well. Attempt to make the process easy on the volunteer teacher.	Ms. Jones has video recorded before and brings her camera to the school the week she plans to film the target lesson. Since the practices may run into a second day, she can then video as many days as needed. Ms. Rodriguez also plans to come by to video record to get an extra angle and close-up on the scenes, especially when students will be speaking to each other.
Step 5: Once the video has been recorded, allow time to review it and clip/excerpt those scenes that will be useful to the planned professional development. Naming conventions and tagging the clip will make it easier to retrieve for later use within a video library. The focus teacher should receive acknowledgement and recognition for their professional contribution.	Ms. Jones provides the video she has taken on a USB stick, and Ms. Rodriguez plans to take some time to review the footage and excerpt what will be useful for the professional development session. She finds the practices she wants and even others she hadn't asked for but which are evident in the clip, so she stores and names those files to use in future sessions. She then shares the clips she is planning to use with Ms. Jones, so she can approve them and feel comfortable with what will be shared. Finally, Ms. Rodriguez uploads the clips, now labeled and tagged, into the district video library. Ms. Rodriguez ensures that a letter thanking Ms. Jones for her service to professional development in the district is signed by the superintendent and placed in her file.

Once teachers are willing to begin video recording their practices for reflection, turning that process toward filming proactively can begin to occur. In a series of sessions, for example, when teachers are sharing clips, they can discuss what they want to film for, then capture that video, and share it at a subsequent session. When carried out preemptively, facilitators can ask for lesson plans, student work, teachers' written commentary, and other artifacts and are more likely to be able to attach those to the video records rather than trying to find those after the fact. These video records and documents can all begin to enrich and form a vibrant video library of teaching.

HOUSING AND STORING A VIDEO LIBRARY OF TEACHING

The most usable video libraries are ones that are simple to use and build on familiar processes or platforms. They are best managed by a single person or group to ensure that the tagging and file naming protocols are consistent. When many educators will be accessing the video library, it is important also that there is professional development as to how to utilize the library and its features. Users should be encouraged to create, cultivate, and curate their own contributions to the library, so it can continuously grow and expand to meet more and more user needs.

Getting Started: Taking time to look at video libraries online and at other institutions is a great way to get a feel for what will be useful and feasible. Even if those libraries are subscription based, it is worthwhile to just look at a sample to get ideas about the way the page is laid out, the search features operate, the amount of text accompanying the videos, and supplementary materials are organized. For instance, with a free trial subscription, the extensive video library of the National Board for Professional Teaching Standards, ATLAS, can be perused (https://www.nbpts.org/atlas/).

Creating a Site: Features available in professional websites can be approximated using local web design tools, such as the one created by a Teaching English to Speakers of Other Languages (TESOL) teacher education program at Hunter College's School of Education using Google Sites (https://sites.google.com/).

Consider a simple homepage that makes its contents clear

Use tabs to separate different video collections

Wherever possible, include accompanying artifacts with the videos

Create video libraries that are relevant to particular areas or divisions to make them smaller and more manageable

Using a Google for Education account to create a site has several benefits: The accounts are password protected, so videos that are stored there within the educational institution can be FERPA compliant; the sites are free, and the tools array is simple and template based; and whatever is updated in the folders that are linked to the site will automatically update the site itself.

Hosting the Collection Online: Another approach is to utilize a web platform designed to host videos available online; each has different features that may be useful depending on the purposes of the video library.

- ***Vimeo*** (https://vimeo.com/) is a site in which collections of videos can be organized. It can be embedded into learning management systems such as Blackboard and allows the user to set various privacy controls on each video.

- *Voicethread* (https://voicethread.com/) allows for videos to be viewed by a group of observers who can participate in discussions with chat or voice.

- *Vialogues* (https://vialogues.com/) enables the viewer to stop and add notes that are linked to timestamps on the video. A threaded conversation can ensue that makes this platform particularly useful for coach/teacher interactions.

Sites such as YouTube are not generally recommended because of the lack of ability to set a password for all members of the community and the interruption of commercial advertising.

Creating a Lexicon for Searches: Once videos and accompanying artifacts are archived in a video library, it is essential that time is spent in determining the search terms that can be used to "tag" the materials. To ensure that the library does not explode into dozens of idiosyncratic search terms, a single lexicon should be made that is used with the materials. For instance, subject matter, grade level, and type of instruction could seem "obvious," yet specific search terms for these should be made explicit, for the local users. Use of a menu of observable teacher and student behaviors should also be included, such as "General Foci for Classroom Observation" provided in Chapter 2.

Keep in Mind

- All videos and accompanying materials must have been obtained with consent, so a process for ensuring parental/guardian consent for minors as well as usage agreement for the adults in the videos should be in place before a video library is built. See Chapter 4 for more details on this process along with sample permission forms.

- Entrance portals for video collections ideally have a user agreement page, such as the one at the Teaching & Learning Exploratory (TLE) based at the University of Michigan School of Education (https://tle.soe.umich.edu/). This asks viewers to agree and acknowledge statements related to reporting any violations of privacy of those in the videos, not sharing passwords, and maintaining a respectful attitude toward the teachers and teaching presented in the cases.

- A process for vetting the videos and materials, preparing them for upload, and tagging them for retrieval should be in place so that the video library is well curated rather than a digital file cabinet. A few, carefully selected materials are much more useful than a multitude of videos that have not been well screened.

- Soliciting feedback from users to report on which videos they found helpful and how they were used with sample video analysis activities could become part of a robust professional development team.

With attention to particular professional development needs and context, a video library can be made up of links to online resources as well as locally produced video records.

PUTTING IDEAS INTO ACTION

Looking across the ideas and activities presented in this chapter, consider the following questions:

1. What do you see as useful in your work in creating a video library of teaching? How might it benefit your colleagues?

2. Which of the six considerations in selecting video materials were new for you? What do you now think would be important for you when selecting video materials to use when facilitating video analysis tasks?

3. Where do you see the distinction of creating, cultivating, and curating video helpful in creating a collection of videos you can use?

4. What other sites have you turned to for finding useful videos of teaching?

5. Which parts of this chapter resonate for you in terms of facilitating other educators' conversations or for your own use of video analysis?

FINAL THOUGHTS: VIDEO ANALYSIS AT WORK

This text offers a variety of precautions, understandings, and suggestions to support the facilitation of video analysis and provides a variety of learning tasks. Framing these tasks within a context shows that there are many ways video analysis can be incorporated into individual teachers' learning as well as at program and institutional levels. Below are some charts that offer examples of how video analysis activities can be used very effectively; these approaches can always be adapted for your needs.

Starting video analysis as early as possible in the teacher career pathway is ideal. When video analysis of teaching is a routine part of their teacher education, teachers enter the profession with the background, experience, and comfort level to much more readily take up video analysis in the workplace. This in turn makes video analysis more fruitful and productive, as teachers continue to learn in their own classrooms.

Beginning with the teacher education setting, Context A below outlines the way video analysis could be woven throughout a teacher education program at the institutional level. Presented in an ideal sequence, the final stage would loop back to the first, providing ever-more relevant video footage for use in illustrating methods to novice teacher learners. Any one of these activities could also stand alone.

CONTEXT A. USE OF VIDEO FOR TEACHER LEARNING IN TEACHER EDUCATION

Teacher candidates view video of methods in their field while in early coursework, guided by faculty.	College supervisors view video in order to develop a shared understanding of observation rubrics and to calibrate their scoring, guided by faculty and clinical experience coordinators.	College supervisors and cooperating teachers watch video of teaching and video of feedback sessions to strengthen their conferencing skills, guided by faculty and clinical experience coordinators.
Teacher candidates collect video of the classroom in early fieldwork and analyze it in class, guided by faculty.	Cooperating teachers learn about mentoring by viewing videos of feedback sessions, guided by clinical teacher educators.	Student teachers share video with peers and classmates in seminar, guided by faculty.
Student teachers video their own practice and share it with peers, guided by one another and faculty-developed protocols.	Student teachers video their observation visits and reflect on their teaching goals, guided by a college field supervisor.	Video clips from student teachers, alumni, and fieldwork are cultivated to include in a video library of teaching to be used in future coursework. Faculty can review video to continue to develop their shared professional vision.

Once teachers are in the workplace, video analysis can be carried out autonomously by interested teachers as individuals, in collegial professional learning circles, in consultation with supervisors, or as part of larger-scale innovations or instructional initiatives.

The scenarios presented in Context B diagrams below present possible options for use by teachers as they continuously grow and improve as reflective practitioners in their workplaces.

CONTEXT B. USE OF VIDEO FOR TEACHER LEARNING IN SCHOOLS

Individual Teacher Learning

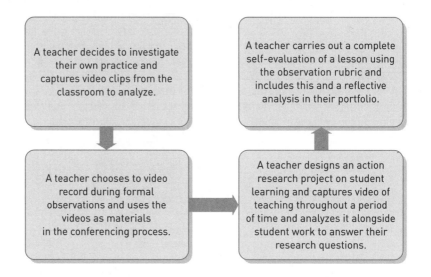

Peer-to-Peer Teacher Learning

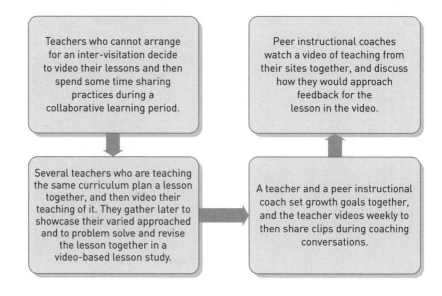

Administration/Supervisor/Trainer/ Coach-Led Teacher Learning

School leaders encourage teachers to video their own practice and share their noticings in a professional learning community (PLC).	Principals invite seasoned, highly effective teachers to opt into a video-based self-evaluation as one of their formal observations.	A coach sets up a PLC focused on student work and includes some video from the teaching to accompany the student work as material for analysis.
Supervisors invite teachers to video during observation visits and then hold off on post-observation conferences until after the teacher has had a chance to review the video.	School leaders engage in "virtual" learning walks by inviting groups of educators to review clips of teaching rather than physically visit classrooms.	Principals in a district participate in calibration training led by district leaders, using video records of lessons from the district and the local observation rubric.
Teachers opt into a PLC that is focused on a particular challenge in their setting. For a series of 8 meetings, a coach facilitates their sharing of short clips from their classrooms as they work to address this challenge.	Teachers in low-incidence subject areas are set up with distance coaches for bi-weekly feedback sessions based on videos of their teaching.	Supervisors video record their own post-observation sessions and review these with school leaders to ensure their feedback skills are supportive to teacher learning.

Video analysis is a powerful tool for teacher learning. Through my various roles and over the course of my 25 years in schools and teacher education, I have come to believe it is the most potent element in transformative teacher learning. Whether it is used to illustrate practice, develop noticing skills, offer exemplary or not-so-exemplary models, or to offer feedback on my own and others' practice, it can enrich learning like no other material.

Video analysis challenges our assumptions, pushes our thinking, and deepens self-awareness, leading ultimately to the professionalization and empowerment of teachers. For teachers to be able to "see" their classrooms honestly and directly is essential for building capacity and sustaining authentic growth. For those who facilitate teacher learning, video analysis could well be thought of as a dynamite stick—volatile, powerful, highly motivating, and effective but only when carefully and thoughtfully handled.

INDEX

A SAGE Publishing Company

Helping educators make the greatest impact

CORWIN HAS ONE MISSION: to enhance education through intentional professional learning.

We build long-term relationships with our authors, educators, clients, and associations who partner with us to develop and continuously improve the best evidence-based practices that establish and support lifelong learning.

THE PROFESSIONAL LEARNING ASSOCIATION

Learning Forward is a nonprofit, international membership association of learning educators committed to one vision in K–12 education: Excellent teaching and learning every day. To realize that vision, Learning Forward pursues its mission to build the capacity of leaders to establish and sustain highly effective professional learning. Information about membership, services, and products is available from www.learningforward.org.